C0-AKZ-790

Exploring Writing Workshop
in the K–2 Classroom:
Discovering Our VOICES

EDUCATION RESOURCE CENTER
University of Delaware
Newark, DE 19716-2940

Exploring Writing Workshop in the K–2 Classroom: Discovering Our VOICES

Debbie Rickards
and
Shirl Hawes

EDUCATION RESOURCE CENTER
University of Delaware
Newark, DE 19716-2940

T 94956

Christopher-Gordon Publishers, Inc.
Norwood, Massachusetts

Copyright Acknowledgments

Every effort has been made to contact copyright holders for permission to reproduce borrowed material where necessary. We apologize for any oversights and would be happy to rectify them in future printings.

All student work reprinted with permission.

Copyright © 2003 by Christopher-Gordon Publishers, Inc.

All rights reserved. Except for review purposes, no part of this material protected by this copyright notice may be reproduced or utilized in any form or by any means, electronic or mechanical, including photocopying, recording, or in any information and retrieval system, without the express written permission of the publisher or copyright holder.

Christopher-Gordon Publishers, Inc.
1502 Providence Highway, Suite #12
Norwood, Massachusetts 02062
800-934-8322
781-762-5577

Printed in the United State of America
10 9 8 7 6 5 4 3 2 1   07 06 05 04 03

ISBN: 1-929024-58-4
Library of Congress Catalogue Number: 2003101601

Contents

Dedication

To our moms—

Martha Arbs and Betty Worcester

Acknowledgments

We owe a special thanks to the people who have contributed to our personal and professional development as we have worked on this manuscript. First, we sincerely appreciate our families who have supported our efforts to become better writing teachers. We thank Josh Hawes for his careful management of our Web site. To our colleagues at Rita Drabek and Boone Elementary Schools, our heartfelt appreciation for your contributions to our professional thinking. Beverly Bollinger, Kerry Laster, and Carol Hankins were supportive principals from our earlier years. We offer a special thank you to our current administrators, Mary Laster and Judy Priest, for supporting and sustaining our professional growth. In addition, our colleagues in our local TABLE group, especially our leader Kathy Spiech, have helped us hone our craft as writing teachers. Finally, we owe a large debt of gratitude to Sue Canavan and Kate Liston at Christopher-Gordon as they have shepherded us through our writing of this text.

Introduction

"Ms Hawes, I've found alliteration and two similes in this poem!" one student excitedly shares. Another student writes, "I was standing in front of the anaconda cage one day. It was slithering across the floor." Both instances were cause for celebration in Shirl's first-grade class. They helped Shirl see that her writing instruction is successful—in garnering students' excitement about writing, in helping them locate writing elements in literature and in poetry, and in facilitating their use of craft elements in their own independent writing. Her students' writing competence has come about because of Shirl's use of VOICES as an instructional framework.

In the fall of 2000, Debbie and Shirl both attended the Texas State Reading Association conference in Dallas. One of the presentations we heard deepened our understanding of quality writing instruction. The presenters, Kathy Stuart and Paula Groberg, shared an instructional idea that used the acronym DIMPLES to help intermediate students focus on the qualities of good writing. After experimenting with their ideas, we revised and reorganized the composition skills for use with primary students. In this text, we'll describe how we use the acronym VOICES to extend our writing instruction.

This book is meant as a resource that can be used by experienced writing teachers as a practical reference when planning writing lessons. The information presented within is a reworking and expansion of one of the chapters from our first book, *Primarily Writing: A Practical Guide for Teachers of Young Children* (Rickards and Hawes, 2003). Our first book covers the theoretical aspects of writing instruction; we have omitted theoretical discussions from this text.

We recommend that you present these VOICES lessons after you have other aspects of writing workshop firmly in place. We include a sequence of instruction, lesson ideas, enrichment options, literature and poetry connections, student samples, and all the ready-to-use materials you'll need to implement the VOICES enrichment lessons in your classroom. We've purposely kept each chapter fairly short to make it more user friendly and doable.

Rather than offering a prescriptive formula, we provide information for our readers that we hope will support and enrich individual writing programs. We don't intend for the information we offer to be a rigid recipe for writing instruction. Instead, we provide explicit examples and direct conversations specifically from Shirl's practice as illustrations of what occurs in our classrooms. Conversations within are meant to be illustrative of how our language sounds as we teach our students; they are not intended as a script. We recommend that you try the lessons presented here using your own language and examples so that you can make it your own and meet the particular needs and interests of your students. In addition, we have a Web site, www.primarilywriting.com, to share new understandings and more instructional ideas related to VOICES and primary writing workshop.

We've structured this book with the intent to provide:

- Use of familiar nursery rhymes to teach writing strategies
- Rhyming couplets with an instructional focus
- Age-appropriate lessons that build on one another
- Plenty of examples of teacher talk, modeling, and guided practice
- Literature and poetry connections
- Reproducible materials

We hope that your writing program will be enriched by the ideas presented in this text. Good luck as you experiment with VOICES and improve the writing of your young students.

Chapter

1

Initiating Writing
Workshop with VOICES

"Is it writing workshop time yet?" Michael asks his teacher as he returns from spring break. "I've got a whole week to write about!" Though he's only a first grader, Michael is thoroughly aware of the power of daily writing. He's eager to write about his vacation, and he clearly sees himself as an author. Michael's motivation and attitude exemplify the kind of primary student who has been immersed in writing workshop.

Both of us, Debbie and Shirl, are primary teachers. In this book, we will share some of the routines that have helped make our students excellent writers. Our intent is to provide explicit instruction and explicit examples from our own practice as we introduce an instructional framework called VOICES that we've designed to extend our routine practices during writing workshop.

VOICES

VOICES is an acronym that stands for the particular elements of a writer's craft (see Figure 1.1). The framework of VOICES has helped us make accessible those writing skills that have often been thought of as out-of-reach of primary writers, such as the use of dialogue, metaphors, and transition words. By systematically and explicitly teaching these craft elements, our primary students' writing has significantly improved. Chapters 2–8 will explain how we use VOICES to enrich our primary writing workshop.

Craft Elements	
V	Vivid Word Choice (strong verbs, leads, and endings)
O	Onomatopoeia and Alliteration
I	Interesting Dialogue and Interjections
C	Comparisons (similes, metaphors, and personification)
E	Expand One Idea (narrow a topic, expand, use transition words) and Emotions
S	Specificity (descriptive words and proper nouns)

Figure 1.1 VOICES Craft Elements

Ongoing Routines

Before beginning our VOICES format, we establish a number of writing routines that are ongoing throughout the year. We'll give a brief description of each element here; for more information, see our book entitled *Primarily Writing: A Practical Guide for Teachers of Young Children* (Rickards and Hawes, 2003). We recommend that you use the VOICES format after mastering these other aspects of writing instruction. In fact, Shirl doesn't even begin VOICES until November of each year. Throughout the year, VOICES lessons are interspersed with other lessons related to writing workshop, including procedures, written conventions, and writer's craft.

Daily Writing Workshop

Children become more proficient at writing by practicing often. They lose momentum if they only write once in a while. Therefore, it's important to make writing workshop a daily routine. Writing workshop has three parts: the mini-lesson, sustained writing, and response time. Mini-lessons are brief coaching sessions where the teacher helps develop the skills and strategies that students need so that they can participate more fully during writing workshop. The lessons we describe in this book are conducted for 5–10 minutes at the beginning of each writing workshop session. After the mini-lesson, students have sustained time to work on their writing. During this part of writing workshop, the teacher is working with individuals and small groups. At the end of writing workshop, 5–10 minutes are devoted to sharing and responding to several students' writing.

Modeling

The teacher is the most powerful model for writing. Throughout the school year, the teacher writes in front of the class. She models topic selection, planning, revising, spelling, editing, and many others skills for her young learners. Though it feels uncomfortable at first, writing in front of others gets easier over time. Most importantly, students reap the rewards of having a teacher who clearly demonstrates what writers do as they compose a text.

Choice

Choice of topics is essential so that students have ownership of an idea and are motivated to write well. When a teacher selects the topics, students often lack the background knowledge or inspiration to develop the teacher's topic. They respond with contrived writing and in an unenthusiastic manner. By allowing students to choose their topics, however, their writing will dramatically improve. We recognize that some schools, districts, and states require students to write to a prompt. If this is true for you, we recommend that prompted writing be a small part of your total writing program.

Five-Page Books

"Five-page books" is an arrangement that we've found extremely helpful for our primary writers. They are simply five pages of paper stapled into a construction paper cover. Writing on one topic, students compose and illustrate using this format. Students use the first page for the beginning of their writing, the next three pages for the middle of their piece, and the last page for the end of the writing. If students have a topic that requires more than five pages, they can easily remove the staples and insert extra sheets. This format is not meant to be a structure in which students complete page one on Monday, page two on Tuesday, and so forth. Instead, five-page books allow for flexibility and encourage students to progress at a pace appropriate for their own development. Writing in five-page books is a continuous process. Once a student finishes one book, another is begun.

Signals to the Reader

We explicitly teach students about the conventions of writing, such as punctuation, left to right progression, and spaces between words. We call these conventions "signals to the reader" because they are used to help readers easily make meaning. Primary students need to know that there is a communicative purpose behind the conventions that all writers use.

Target Skills

We've found that our students' writing skills have increased when we paid more attention to using modeling and direct instruction in the specific skills that we want student to use. Target skills are the skills and strategies that writers use to write well—skills used when organizing, composing, elaborating, and revising a written piece. Target skills may be as basic as beginning a sentence with a capital letter or as complex as crafting a satisfying ending. We use a target and arrows (see Figure 1.2) to encourage our students to "hit the writing target."

Figure 1.2   Sample Target With Target Skill

Target Practice

"Target practice" is a quick exercise where students practice using a target skill isolated from their current work in a five-page book. We use target practice to check for each student's understanding of a particular target skill. We first introduce a target skill, share examples from literature, and model its use. Then we give the students a half-sheet of paper and invite them to practice applying the target skill. Once students have completed the assigned target practice, they go back to their five-page book. We do a quick assessment to see who may need further help applying the target skill. We then pull a small group of students who need more support, reteach the skill, and write a sample sentence together. We include many examples of target practice within the following chapters.

Use of Literature and Poetry

Although the teacher is the most powerful model of writing skills and strategies, literature and poetry can also be used to help students become more thoughtful writers. Our mini-lessons contain a literature and/or poetry component so that we can help the students learn how published authors deal with different aspects of a writer's craft. For example, if we wanted our students to see how an author uses descriptive words to describe the setting, we might examine several pages from Faith Ringgold's (1991) *Tar Beach*. By examining well-written books and poems, teachers help students focus on the many qualities of good writing.

Systematic Assessment and Small Group Instruction

We assess so that we can determine progress and assign grades, of course, but the most important reason is to guide our instruction. By considering developmental levels, comparisons to grade level objectives, and achievement on target skills through the use of rubrics, we are able to use the information gained through each assessment to plan future mini-lessons. Additionally, we can use our assessment data to design small group instruction focused on specific needs. While most students are working on their sustained writing tasks, we often pull a group of children who need instruction on a particular writing skill or strategy. We collect student work in portfolios to help the children and us assess their progress over time.

Response Activities

In our classrooms, we have several structures that support our young writers' need to interact and share their writing with others. We know that writers need to talk with others throughout the writing process as they craft a piece. We also know that responses from their peers and the teacher help writers discover what they do or do not understand, what they have and have not tried, and what they are or are not communicating in their writing. We devise opportunities for our students to share with one another, respond to each other's writing, get feedback from each other and from us, and reflect on their writing based upon their interaction with others. Response opportunities occur through an Author's Chair ritual, partner sharing time, and peer and teacher-led conferences.

Chapter

2   Hearing Our VOICES

As we've used five-page books and target skills with our young writers, we felt like we were competent writing teachers. Our students were learning writing skills and strategies and loving writing workshop. But to move our teaching skills from competence to excellence, we needed something more. VOICES has allowed us to take our writing instruction to a higher level.

VOICES as an Organizational Tool

VOICES stands for elements of a writer's craft that we've found useful in teaching young writers. *V* signifies vivid word choice, *O* means onomatopoeia, *I* stands for interesting dialogue, *C* is for comparisons, *E* indicates expansion of one idea, and *S* represents specificity. Within each letter category are several skills that we explicitly teach (see Figure 2.1). We first spend time teaching the skills of vivid word choice. Then, while periodically reviewing elements previously studied, we move on to the skills under *O,* then *I,* and so on. For each letter category, we use an illustrative icon and sample sentence. Each skill within the six categories has a rhyming couplet to help define the skill and to assist students in remembering the craft element. We also use nursery rhymes, popular poetry, and literature connections to help students identify and practice the target skills under VOICES. (Unless otherwise noted, the poems we suggest in this book were selected from *The Random House Book of Poetry for Children* [Prelutsky, 1983].) In addition, we devote a large bulletin board to VOICES, where we display the letter, icon, sample sentence, rhyming couplets, and assorted samples from literature and from students' writing (see Figure 2.2).

	Stands for . . .	Target Skills Included	Sample Sentences
V	Vivid Word Choice	Strong verbs, leads, and endings	The frog leaped over the log.
O	Onomatopoeia	Onomatopoeia and alliteration	Splash! The duck dives deep into the pond.
I	Interesting Dialogue	Interesting dialogue and interjections	"Wow! Look at that bug," said Tom. Billy said, "It's a big cricket."
C	Comparisons	Similes, metaphors, and personification	The rain played a sad song on my head. My hair felt like a wet mop.
E	Expand One Idea	Expand one idea, narrow the topic, use transition words, and evoke emotions	Suddenly, a door creaked open. Out slithered an enormous dragon.
S	Specificity	Descriptive words and proper nouns	Rover found two big bones under the wooden table.

Figure 2.1   VOICES Framework

Figure 2.2   VOICES Bulletin Board

We follow these lessons in the sequence presented in our VOICES framework, although presenting them in any order would be fine. We recommend that first-grade teachers devote approximately 1 month per letter and that second grade teachers spend 1–2 weeks on each letter as a review. If your second-grade students are unfamiliar with the VOICES format, however, 1 month per letter would be appropriate. Kindergarten teachers can use the VOICES framework, too. One letter per 6 weeks would be about right for kindergartners, but we recommend that kindergarten teachers utilize only the literature component of these lessons. Kindergartners are unlikely to be developmentally ready to integrate the VOICES lessons into their own writing, though teachers can utilize the lessons during modeled writing activities. We do VOICES lessons once or twice a week; the other days are devoted to mini-lessons designed in response to student needs, as determined by our routine assessment.

Before you are ready to introduce each letter and its components, you'll need to prepare several graphics to use with each lesson. We find that reproducing these graphics on card stock and then laminating them increases durability. For each letter, you'll need posters of the letter, broad

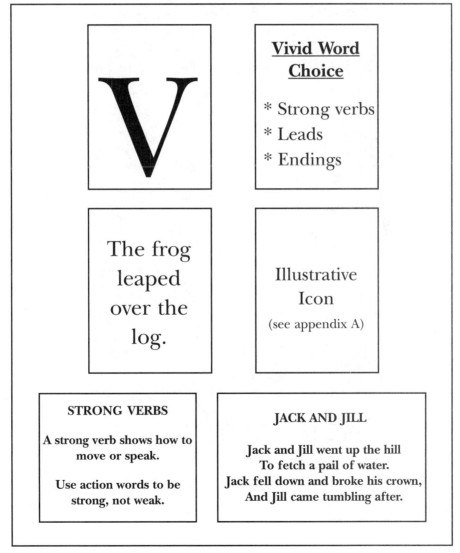

Figure 2.3 Graphics of a VOICES Lesson

skill, icon, sample sentence, and rhyming couplets, all printed on 8 ½ x 11-inch paper. For many lessons, you'll also need nursery rhymes reproduced on chart paper or on a transparency. (All necessary components are available for reproduction in the appendices.) You'll learn more about these components as we describe our lessons. Figure 2.3 illustrates the graphics necessary for introducing strong verbs (a subset of vivid word choice). In Figure 2.4, you see two sections of a completed VOICES board. In addition to the teacher-made graphics, there are also class-made charts, student samples, examples from literature, and comic strips displayed on the board.

Figure 2.4   Sections of the VOICES Board

VOICES Lessons

Our VOICES mini-lessons introduce each skill using a rhyming couplet, followed by discussion, modeling, literature connections, and guided practice. Many of the lessons have a target practice component. As students find and create samples of each skill, they post them on the VOICES bulletin board. After each mini-lesson, students continue work in their five-page books. We encourage our students to use the VOICES skills in their own books, and we celebrate as we see students independently using each VOICES skill. The following chapters explain all the craft elements included within the VOICES format. Using Shirl's first-grade class as an example, we take you lesson-by-lesson as the VOICES activities are developed and enriched. As we've said before, we don't intend that the information we offer is a prescriptive recipe for writing instruction. Instead, we provide explicit examples from Shirl's first-grade classroom as illustrations of what occurs in our classrooms. Her conversations within this text are meant to be illustrative of how her language sounds as she teaches her students; they are not intended as a script. We recommend that you try the lessons presented here using your own language and examples so that you can make it your own and meet the particular needs and interests of your students.

Chapter

3   Vivid Word Choice

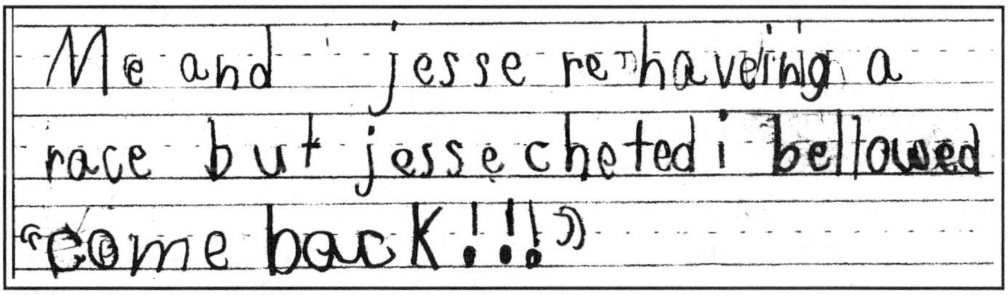

Me and jesse re having a race but jesse choted i bellowed "come back!!!"

Figure 3.1 Joel's Writing

Shirl's first graders are avid writers. Their personalities shine through in their writing, and they willingly take chances by trying new and different craft techniques. Joel's writing, seen in the figure above, illustrates how he experiments with precise word choice as he chooses the word "bellowed" to express his anger when Jesse cheated during their race. In this chapter, we will see how Shirl helps her students expand their vocabularies and extend the ways they communicate their ideas through vivid word choice.

As we introduce this VOICES category, we include the target skills of strong verbs, good leads, and appealing endings. We use the sentence "The frog leaped over the log" as a sample sentence for vivid words. We also use the picture of a frog jumping over a log as an accompanying illustration (see appendix A). (You can, of course, make up your own sample sentence with a corresponding picture for this and all the examples presented in this book.)

Strong Verbs

Introductory Lessons

The skill of strong verbs is introduced and practiced for 1–2 weeks. Several introductory mini-lessons are necessary first, and then you and your students practice identifying strong verbs until you think that most students have mastered the concept and are ready to move on.

Lesson 1 begins as the students gather on the floor around Shirl in her large-group seating area. Shirl holds up the 8 ½ x 11-inch poster of the *V*. She says, "Today we are going to learn about something good writers do to make their pieces better. It's called vivid word choice, which means using words that give readers a good picture in their heads. The *V* stands for vivid word choice." She shows students the sample sentence and says, "Here's a sentence that uses vivid word choice or exciting words. Let's read it together." After reading, Shirl asks, "What picture came into your head when you heard those words?" Students respond, and then Shirl displays the picture icon. "Here is a picture to remind us to use vivid or exciting words. It's just like the picture you saw in your head." Shirl leads the students in observing that *leaped* is a good word choice because it gives the reader specific information, and it helps the reader to visualize the author's meaning.

Shirl's lesson continues, "When we listen to stories and poems over the next few days, we're going to be detectives searching for interesting action words. Action words are called verbs, so we'll be looking for words that give us a strong picture of the action. We'll call them strong verbs. When we find them, we'll write them on this chart." Shirl introduces the rhyming couplet (see Figure 3.2) and teaches the kinesthetic movement corresponding to vivid word choice—students make a *V* with two fingers when they hear a strong verb. She says, "I have a little poem that will help you to remember about strong verbs. When you hear a strong verb, you can think of the poem and hold up your fingers in a V to show that you're a good word detective." Shirl then reads a short book, and the students listen for vivid verbs. If they hear one, they hold up the V sign. After the story is complete, they add the strong words they heard to the chart. If her students don't hear a strong verb in the selection, Shirl says, "I heard a strong verb on this page. Listen when I read it again and put up a V sign when you hear it." We recommend that you do this verb search in moderation. You don't want to interrupt every page of the story!

Lesson 2 begins with a review of the target skill and accompanying sample sentence, icon, and rhyming couplet. Shirl then continues the lesson by stating, "Today we're going to practice our target skill by using the nursery rhyme *Jack and Jill.*" Shirl and her students read the poem

---

STRONG VERBS

A strong verb shows how to move or speak.
Use action words to be strong, not weak.

Figure 3.2 Rhyming Couplet for Strong Verbs

that's been written on chart paper. She then says, "When someone wrote this nursery rhyme, they used the word *went* to show how Jack and Jill moved up the hill. That's not a very strong verb! It doesn't tell us exactly *how* they moved up the hill. Did they march? Did they crawl? Did they skip? Let's see if we can think of other words that would give us a better picture of how Jack and Jill went up the hill." As students offer suggestions, the class recites the first line of *Jack and Jill*, substituting a strong verb for *went*. As each suggestion is read, Shirl and her students act out the suggested movement (including slithering on the floor!).

Shirl spends another day or two working with other nursery rhymes as the children substitute strong verbs for the verb in the rhyme. Suggestions include *The Bear Went Over the Mountain* (changing the verb *went*) and *Jack Be Nimble* (changing the verb *jumped* in the phrase "Jack jumped over the candlestick").

In the third mini-lesson, students practice the target skill by writing a sentence with a strong verb. First they review the sample sentence, icon, and rhyming couplet. Shirl continues, "Today we're going to do our target practice. We're each going to write a sentence that has a strong verb. We want to make sure that we use a word that makes a clear picture in our readers' minds." Shirl writes the sentence "I went down the street" to model how to give the reader a better picture. "In this sentence, I used the word *went*. Does that tell my reader how I moved as I went down the street? What's a word that would be better?" Shirl then crosses out *went* and writes a new choice. She asks, "What other words would make sense and give the reader a better picture?" After a discussion, Shirl says, "Now it's your turn to try to hit the target! You can use my frame sentence, 'I ____ down the street,' or you can make up a sentence of your own and use a strong verb. After you write a sentence, you illustrate it. Bring it to me when you're finished, and then begin working on your five-page book. You might find a place in your five-page book where you can use a strong verb." Shirl passes out paper for the target practice, and the students return to their seats to write a sentence including a strong verb. An example of this target practice is shown in Figure 3.3. As children turn in their target practice, Shirl quickly checks the work and helps students who are struggling with the target skill. To close the lesson, Shirl asks several students to read their target practice sentences to the class, and then they chant the rhyming couplet. Finally, Shirl says, "Tomorrow during writing workshop, when you feel your pencil writing a boring verb like *went* or *go*, think about switching to a strong verb to tell your reader *how* to move."

Figure 3.3   Strong Verbs Target Practice

Shirl's next mini-lesson focuses on substitutions for *said*. The format of this lesson is similar to the lesson using *Jack and Jill*. For this lesson, Shirl and her students first review the rhyming couplet for strong verbs. She then introduces the rhyme *Five Little Monkeys Jumping on the Bed*. After reading the rhyme, students consider substitutions for the word *said* in the line, "The doctor said, 'No more monkeys jumping on the bed.'" They repeat the line using alternative words with corresponding voices (e.g., *whispered, bellowed, shouted, screamed*), and Shirl writes them on stick-on notes (see Figure 3.4).

The next day Shirl and her students review the previous day's lesson, and then they practice the target skill on their own. Shirl models with the sentence "Mom said, 'Go to bed.'" She tells the students that they can either use her frame sentence, "Mom ____, 'Go to bed,'" or they can write a sentence of their own, using a strong verb as a replacement for *said.* (Shirl will teach the punctuation that accompanies dialogue later in the year.) Student sentences should include who is talking (e.g., mom, dad, teacher, or friend), what they are saying (e.g., go to bed, clean up, or put your head down), and how they are saying it (e.g., with a scream, whisper, or cry).

Figure 3.4 Substitutions for *Said*

Accomplished writers practice moderation in their use of strong verbs. Moderation is a difficult concept for first and second graders to understand, so you will want to be careful how you model and support the use of this skill. We try to encourage students to use one strong verb per page by thinking about which action they really want to make distinctive. If there are too many strong verbs in a piece, the writing sounds artificial and unnatural.

As these lessons are occurring, Shirl and her first graders begin collecting examples of strong verbs to display on the VOICES bulletin board. Shirl contributes cartoons that she has cut out of the newspaper. She copies target practice sentences to add to the display. If students find a good example of a strong verb, they recopy it and contribute it to the display, too (as shown in Figure 2.2). When children independently add a strong verb to their writing (see Figure 3.5), Shirl also displays it on the VOICES board. Collections such as these become routine for each component of the VOICES lessons.

Figure 3.5 Independent Use of Strong Verbs

Enrichment Activities

Simon Says is a fun game to play to help reinforce strong verbs. This game is played in the standard way, only Simon's commands are strong verbs. As examples, if the leader says, "Simon says 'shout your name,'" the rest of the students shout their names. But if the leader just says, "bellow your name," the students do not follow the command.

After reading the poem "Follow the Leader" (from *The Random House Book of Poetry for Children* [Prelutsky, 1983]), Shirl plays *Follow the Leader* with her students. She forms a single line (it's good to do this outside!); the first person leads the line and says a strong verb. The rest of the line follows and performs the action indicated by the verb. After several turns, a new leader is selected.

The games of *Simon Says* and *Follow the Leader* described above were done orally. Shirl also plays these same games with written verbs. She has her students each write a strong verb on an index card. The cards are placed in a bag, and then the leader of each game selects a command from the bag to read to the class.

Using the character cards and strong verbs spinner found in appendix C, Shirl teaches an activity called *Strong Verbs Spin*. To prepare for the activity, Shirl first copies the character cards, laminates them, cuts them apart, and then stores them in a paper gift bag on which she has glued large wiggly eyes from a craft store (see Figure 3.6). She also copies the spinner, mounts it on poster board, and laminates it. To do Strong Verbs Spin, a student inserts a pencil into one end of a large paper clip and places the pencil point in the center of the spinner. This action creates the spinner, which the student then spins, landing either on the rabbit or the turtle on the spinner board. After spinning, the student selects a character card from the bag. The task is then to create a sentence containing the character as the subject coupled with a strong verb (either something the character said or did), depending on the outcome of the spin from the spinner board. For example, if the student selected the *astronaut* from the character bag and the spinner landed on the rabbit, the student might create the sentence, "The astronaut bellowed." If, however, the spinner landed on the turtle, the student might create the sentence, "The astronaut floated." Shirl introduces this activity as a writing workshop mini-lesson and plays it occasionally during writing time. She sometimes requires that the students extend the sentences they create (e.g., What did the astronaut bellow? Where did he float?). She also uses Strong Verbs Spin whenever she has a few extra minutes during transitions (e.g., walking down the hall, lining up for recess, waiting for dismissal); and once the students understand the activity, she transfers it to an independent work station. (The character cards and spinners are suggested as enrichment activities throughout this text. The preparation and procedures are the same for all the activities, regardless of the skill that is reinforced.)

Additional opportunities for enrichment occur throughout the year. By using literature and poems, Shirl routinely helps her students locate the strong verbs within each piece (see Figures 3.7 and 3.8).

Figure 3.6 Bag for Character Cards

LITERATURE TITLES—STRONG VERBS			
Title	**Author**	**Publisher**	**Copyright Date**
Santa Calls	W. Joyce	HarperCollins	1993
To Root, to Toot, to Parachute: What is a Verb?	B. P. Cleary	Carolhoda Books	2001
Tops and Bottoms	J. Stevens	Harcourt Brace	1995
Rockabye Crocodile	J. Aruego & A. Dewey	Greenwillow	1988
Rude Giants	A. Wood	Harcourt Brace	1993
Clap Your Hands	L. B. Cauley	Scholastic	1992
Hush	M. Ho	Orchard	1996
Pretend You're a Cat	J. Marzollo	Scholastic	1990
Puddles	J. London	Scholastic	1997
Time to Sleep	D. Fleming	Scholastic	1997
Into the A. B, Sea	D. L. Rose	Scholastic	2000

Figure 3.7 Literature Titles for Teaching Strong Verbs

POETRY TITLES—STRONG VERBS		
Source: *The Random House Book of Poetry for Children* (Prelutsky, 1983)		
Title	**Author**	**Page Number**
"Mark's Fingers"	Mary O'Neill	120
"Seal"	William Jay Smith	62
"Open Hydrant"	Marci Ridlon	96
"Cat"	Mary Britton Miller	68
"The Hen"	Lord Alfred Douglas	85
"Did You?"	William Cole	106
"We're Racing, Racing Down the Walk"	Phyllis McGinley	111
"Barbershop"	Martin Gardner	113
"Sulk"	Felice Holman	121
"The Alligator"	Mary Macdonald	176
"The Creature in the Classroom"	Jack Prelutsky	212

Figure 3.8 Poetry Titles for Teaching Strong Verbs

Leads

Introductory Lessons

In this lesson sequence, Shirl introduces the meaning and purpose of a lead, teaches students one way to make a good lead, and assists students as they experiment with various leads for the pieces on which they are working.

The first mini-lesson begins with Shirl saying the following, "When I watch a movie, I can usually tell right away if I'm going to like it. The beginning of the movie needs to be interesting and get my attention. Our writing is the same way. The beginning needs to be interesting and get our reader's attention. The first few sentences are called the *lead*. The lead hooks our reader into reading more." Shirl introduces the rhyming couplet (see Figure 3.9), and she and the students chant the rhyme several times. She continues, "One way that we can hook our reader with our lead is to show action. We learned all about action sentences when we talked about strong verbs." The class repeats the rhyming couplet for strong verbs and reviews a few of the sentences on the VOICES bulletin board under "Vivid Word Choice."

LEADS

A good lead is like a hook.
It makes your reader take a look.

Figure 3.9   Rhyming Couplet for Leads

Next, Shirl holds up *Alexander and the Terrible, Horrible, No Good, Very Bad Day* (Viorst, 1972). She says, "We've read this book before. Alexander was having a terrible day! When Judith Viorst wrote this book, she wrote a lead that uses action. Listen to all the action words that she uses in the first page of this book. 'I went to sleep with gum in my mouth and now there's gum in my hair and when I got out of bed this morning I tripped on the skateboard and by mistake I dropped my sweater in the sink while the water was running and I could tell it was going to be a terrible, horrible, no good, very bad day.' Doesn't that lead hook you and make you want to read more? Let's chant our rhyme again." When they are finished chanting, Shirl tells them to continue working on their current five-page books.

For the second mini-lesson on leads, Shirl displays the nursery rhyme *Three Little Kittens*. She reads the first line dramatically in a sobbing voice. "'Three little kittens have lost their mittens and they began to cry.' That lead makes me feel like I'm right there with those sad kittens. It makes me wonder what will happen next to these poor kittens. This nursery rhyme is an example of a piece that uses action as the lead. The action makes me want to keep reading."

Now Shirl is ready to model writing a lead of her own. She says, "In this five-page book, I'm going to write about my dog Shiloh. I want to tell how Shiloh felt when my other dog, Lester, died. I could begin with, 'Shiloh was sad when Lester died.' That's kind of boring, though, and probably won't hook my reader. I'll try to rewrite my lead to show action. How does this sound?" Shirl begins to write in her five-page book, "'Shiloh searched everywhere for Lester and then howled a sad goodbye.' I think those actions will make my readers curious and want to read more. When good writers begin a piece, they try to write a lead that will be interesting and get their readers' attention. When you are beginning a new piece, you'll want to think about using action to hook your reader." The class chants the rhyming couplet for leads again before they continue working on their current five-page books.

The third mini-lesson is used for target practice. Prior to the lesson, Shirl has written the nursery rhyme *Little Bo Beep* on a chart paper or transparency. After the class has said the rhyming couplet for leads and reviewed the previous day's work, she says, "Today for target practice, we're going to use the nursery rhyme *Little Bo Peep*. We're going to experiment with different leads that show action. When we experiment, we try something in a different way. When writers do this, it's called *revision*. They try their writing in a different way. We're going to experiment with the lead for *Little Bo Peep*." Shirl reads the nursery rhyme, and then focuses on the beginning line, "Little Bo Peep has lost her sheep." She continues, "We know that Little Bo Peep has lost her sheep, but we don't know why she lost them. If we were to experiment with a different lead, we could show what she was doing when the sheep got lost. Maybe we could say, 'Little Bo Peep was picking flowers, and then she lost her sheep.' Or we could say, 'Little Bo Peep was reading a book, and then she lost her sheep.' What are some other actions that Little Bo Peep could be doing when the sheep got lost?" As students suggest actions, Shirl writes them on chart paper, which will later be displayed on the VOICES board. After the students have brainstormed some possible actions of Little Bo Peep, Shirl gives them their target practice assignment. "Your job for target practice is to write a new lead that shows Little Bo Peep and her action. You might want to start your sentence with 'Little Bo Peep ___, and then she lost her sheep.'" Shirl writes this phrase on the board and distributes paper for target practice. When students have finished, they return to their five-page book. For students who struggled with the target practice, Shirl holds a small group conference; and they write a new lead together.

The fourth mini-lesson on leads focuses on the students' current pieces. Shirl asks the students to bring the five-page book they're currently working on as they gather on the floor. The class reviews the purpose for a lead and chants the rhyming couplet. Then she says, "Today we're going to look at some of your leads and see if we can experiment to make the lead show action. Who would like to start?" Freddie volunteers and reads his lead: "I like to go roller blading." As two or three students offer suggestions for different leads showing action, Shirl writes their ideas on stick-on notes and gives them to Freddie. After several other students have read their original lead and received suggestions for other options, Shirl closes the mini-lesson by reminding the students that good writers experiment with their writing and often try more than one lead. (Shirl is not expecting Freddie or the other students to go back and use the stick-on notes to revise their leads, however. She keeps in mind that her job is to improve the writer, not the writing. Shirl is giving her students a strategy for improving their leads in future pieces.)

Shirl repeats this lesson a few times with other students' leads. She will revisit the topic of leads at several points later in the VOICES sequence of lessons. As Shirl introduces onomatopoeia, alliteration, dialogue, interjections, and comparison (see Figure 3.10), she shows how these skills can be used as leads.

TYPES OF LEADS

- Action
- Onomatopoeia
- Alliteration
- Dialogue
- Interjection
- Comparison

Figure 3.10 Lead Types Introduced in the VOICES Format

Enrichment Activities

Identifying effective leads occurs throughout the year. During many language arts activities utilizing literature or poetry, Shirl calls attention to the lead and discusses its effectiveness. She sometimes writes a lead sentence and its source on a chart she keeps headed *Lively Leads*. Literature and poetry resources are found in Figures 3.11 and 3.12.

LITERATURE TITLES—LEADS				
Type of Lead	**Title**	**Author**	**Publisher**	**Copyright Date**
Action	*George Shrinks*	W. Joyce	HarperCollins	1985
	Alexander and the Wind-Up Mouse	L. Lionni	Alfred A. Knopf	1969
	Alexander and the Terrible, Horrible, No Good, Very Bad Day	J. Viorst	Aladdin	1972
Onomatopoeia	*Pancakes, Pancakes*	E. Carle	Scholastic	1990
	The Little Engine That Could	W. Piper	Platt & Munk	1954
Alliteration	*Princess Penelope's Parrot*	H. Lester	Houghton Mifflin	1996
	Wemberly Worried	K. Henkes	Greenwillow Books	2000
	Lilly's Purple Plastic Purse	K. Henkes	Greenwillow Books	1996

Figure 3.11 Literature Titles for Teaching Leads   *(Continued on next page)*

LITERATURE TITLES—LEADS				
Type of Lead	Title	Author	Publisher	Copyright Date
Dialogue	*The Doorbell Rang*	P. Hutchins	Scholastic	1986
	Regards to the Man in the Moon	E. J. Keats	Trumpet Club	1981
	No Nap	E. Bunting	Clarion	1989
	Jumanji	C. Van Allsburg	Scholastic	1981
Interjection	*Whistle for Willie*	E. J. Keats	Viking Press	1964
	Amelia Bedelia	P. Parish	Scholastic	1963
Comparison	*Amber on the Mountain*	T. Johnston	Puffin	1994
	Alice Nizzy Nazzy: The Witch of Santa Fe	T. Johnston	G. P. Putnam's Sons	1995

Figure 3.11 Literature Titles for Teaching Leads *(Continued)*

POETRY TITLES—LEADS			
Source: *The Random House Book of Poetry for Children* (Prelutsky, 1983)			
Type of Lead	Title	Author	Page Number
Dialogue	"The Secret Song"	Margaret Wise Brown	24
	"Soap"	Martin Gardner	138
Interjection	"Hey, Bug!"	Lilian Moore	72
Onomatopoeia	"Fishes' Evening Song"	Dahlov Ipcar	78
Action	"Open Hydrant"	Marci Ridlon	96
	"We're Racing, Racing Down the Walk"	Phyllis McGinley	111
	"Sulk"	Felice Holman	121
	"In the Motel"	X. J. Kennedy	137
Alliteration	"Fishes' Evening Song"	Dahlov Ipcar	78
	"Night"	Mary Ann Hoberman	33
	"The Hippopotamus"	Jack Prelutsky	58
	"The Lesser Linx"	E. V. Rieu	60
Comparison	"Flint"	Christina Rossetti	23
	"The Rain Has Silver Sandals"	May Justus	29
	"The Night is a Big Black Cat"	G. Orr Clark	33
	"I've Got a Dog"	Anonymous	66

Figure 3.12 Poetry Titles for Teaching Leads

After students have learned about all the different kinds of leads listed above, Shirl teaches an activity called *Lively Leads Spin*. Using the character cards and the leads spinner from appendix C, she guides her students to create a lead sentence based upon the chosen character and the type of lead selected on the spinner. Examples using *astronaut* as the character include the following:

- Onomatopoeia—Crash! The astronaut dropped the telescope.

- Dialogue—May Day! May Day! My spaceship has crashed!

- Interjection—Oh, no! We're having trouble with the lunar landing!

Endings

Introductory Lessons

To introduce students to appealing endings, Shirl first discusses boring endings. She says, "Raise your hand if you like to be bored. Of course you don't! Readers don't like to be bored either, but sometimes writers write endings that are boring. If a writer writes, 'And then I went home' or 'And then I went to bed,' those endings make me bored. Sometimes writers end with 'And it was all a dream.' Endings like that make me think that the writer didn't know much about writing appealing endings. *Appealing* means interesting. Let's read our rhyme about endings" (see Figure 3.13). After the class has chanted the rhyming couplet, Shirl continues, "Our rhyme tells us three ways to write an appealing ending. When a story ends with a surprise, that's certainly not boring! So a good ending might end with a surprise to the reader. Sometimes authors write a *circle story*. In a circle story, the end circles back and is connected to the beginning. Sometimes writers end their pieces by using feelings. The characters in the story might feel happy or sad. Or the reader might have strong feelings at the end. The end might make the reader feel happy or sad."

ENDINGS

Use a big surprise, a circle, or a feeling.
To write a good ending that's much more appealing.

Figure 3.13 Rhyming Couplet for Endings

Next Shirl displays three books that she has previously read to the class. Each book represents one of the three kinds of endings: surprise, circle, and feeling. In this example, Shirl uses *Flossie and the Fox* (McKissack, 1986), *If You Give a Mouse a Cookie* (Numeroff, 1985), and *Thank You, Mr. Falker* (Polacco, 1998). Shirl says, "We've read these three books before. When we read *Flossie and the Fox,* we were surprised when Flossie tricked the fox. *Flossie and the Fox* is an example of a book with a surprise ending. *If You Give a Mouse a Cookie* has a circle ending. In the beginning, the mouse wanted a glass of milk, and at the end the mouse wants another glass of milk. The story circles back to the beginning. In *Thank You, Mr. Falker,* Patricia Polacco writes an ending that makes us have strong feelings. At the end of this story, we feel really good that Patricia has learned to read. Let's start a chart and write the titles of the books we read and the kinds of endings that they have." Shirl writes the titles of these books on the chart (see Figure 3.14). (This chart will continue to be used throughout the year as the class reads other books and identifies the kind of endings they have. It becomes part of the VOICES bulletin board.) Students chant the rhyming couplet for endings and then continue work on their current five-page books.

Surprise	Circle	Feeling
• *Flossie and the Fox*	• *If You Give a Mouse a Cookie*	• *Thank You, Mr. Falker*

Figure 3.14   Endings Chart

Prior to the next mini-lesson, Shirl has revised the nursery rhyme *Little Miss Muffet* and has written it on chart paper (see Figure 3.15). When her students have gathered for the mini-lesson, Shirl says, "I've rewritten the nursery rhyme *Little Miss Muffet.* Listen to my boring ending." She reads the rhyme to the class, then continues, "Isn't that boring?! When we were writing leads, we said that writers sometimes experiment. Writers will also often try different ways to write an ending. Who can remember three ways to make an appealing ending?" After students recall the three ways, the class chants the rhyming couplet. Shirl wants to help her students experiment with different ways to end her Miss Muffet rhyme. She's not concerned that they identify the type of ending; she just wants them to consider other options. She resumes her mini-lesson. "I'm going to experiment and make up a different ending to replace my boring one.

After the spider sat down beside her, maybe I could end with 'Then that hungry spider gobbled up the curds and whey!' That's a new ending! Or I could write 'Miss Muffet jumped off her tuffet, grabbed a hammer, and squashed that nasty spider flat!' Put your thumbs up if you like my endings. Can anyone else experiment and try a new ending for *Little Miss Muffet*?" The students volunteer ideas for a new ending. The class concludes this lesson by chanting the rhyming couplet.

Little Miss Muffet (revised)

Little Miss Muffet sat on a tuffet
Eating her curds and whey.
Along came a spider
And sat down beside her.
And then Miss Muffet went home.

Figure 3.15   Revision of "Little Miss Muffet"

Enrichment Activities

Other lessons on appealing endings will be spread throughout the school year. As the year progresses, Shirl and her students will identify and chart the types of endings in books that they read. They will collect samples of appealing endings for the VOICES bulletin board. Often after a read aloud book, Shirl will model experimenting with two or three other ending possibilities. The titles in Figures 3.16 and 3.17 are good sources with appealing endings.

Engaging Endings Spin is an activity Shirl uses as a whole group review. She first names a nursery rhyme and then has a student spin the spinner. Depending upon where the spinner lands, the students work together to brainstorm a different ending for the rhyme. Using *Humpty Dumpty* as the nursery rhyme, for example, students might suggest endings as follows:

- Feeling—All the King's men where starving, so they cooked an omelet.

- Surprise—Police are investigating the spider who sat down behind him and scared Humpty Dumpty to death.

- Circle—All the King's men put Humpty together again and sat him up on the wall.

LITERATURE TITLES—ENDINGS				
Type of Ending	Title	Author	Publisher	Copyright Date
Surprise	*The Wednesday Surprise*	E. Bunting	Clarion	1989
	Just Like Daddy	F. Asch	Aladdin	1988
	Just Like Everybody Else	K. Kuskin	HarperCollins	1959
	Flossie and the Fox	P. McKissack	Dial Books for Young Readers	1986
	The Doorbell Rang	P. Hutchins	Scholastic	1986
Circular	*Two Bad Ants*	C. Van Allsburg	Houghton Mifflin	1988
	If You Give a Mouse a Cookie	L. Numeroff	HarperCollins	1985
	The Relatives Came	C. Rylant	Aladdin	1985
Feelings	*Wilfred Gordon McDonald Partridge*	M. Fox	Kane/Miller	1985
	William's Doll	C. Zolotow	HarperCollins	1972
	Thank You, Mr. Falker	P. Polacco	Philomel	1988
	Gorilla	A. Browne	Knopf	1983
	Lost	P. B. Johnson & C. Lewis	Scholastic	1998

Figure 3.16   Literature Titles for Teaching Endings

POETRY TITLES—ENDINGS			
Source: *The Random House Book of Poetry for Children* (Prelutsky, 1983)			
Type of Ending	Title	Author	Page Number
Surprise	"Mother Doesn't Want a Dog"	Judith Viorst	133
	"Did You?"	William Cole	106
	"No Girls Allowed"	Jack Prelutsky	111
Circular	"Mice"	Rose Fyleman	54
	"Wrestling"	Kathleen Fraser	112
Feelings	"April Rain Song"	Langston Hughes	97
	"Ants, Although Admirable, Are Awfully Aggravating"	Walter R. Brooks	74
	"The Bug"	Marjorie Barrows	74

Figure 3.17   Poetry Titles for Teaching Endings

Preparation for Teaching

In each of the remaining chapters, we will end with a list of items that you'll need to prepare for each VOICES component. Many of the things you need to copy are available in the appendices. In addition to what we list here, you'll need classroom supplies such as chart paper, sentence strips, markers, and stick-on notes.

Resources for Lessons

- Posters:
    - –the large letter V
    - –the skills list
    - –the sample sentence
    - –the rhyming couplets for strong verbs, leads, and endings
- Traditional rhymes copied onto transparencies or chart paper:
    - –*Jack and Jill*
    - –*The Bear Went Over the Mountain*
    - –*Jack Be Nimble*
    - –*Five Little Monkeys Jumping on the Bed*
    - –*Three Little Kittens*
    - –*Little Bo Peep*
    - –*Little Miss Muffet* (revised)
- Suggested books:
    - –*Alexander and the Terrible, Horrible, No Good, Very Bad Day (Viorst)*
    - –*Flossie and the Fox (McKissack)*
    - –*If You Give a Mouse a Cookie (Numeroff)*
    - –*Thank You, Mr. Falker (Polacco)*

Resources for Enrichment Activities

- Any book or poem listed in Figures 3.7, 3.8, 3.11, 3.12, 3.16, and 3.17
- Character cards in character bag
- Spinners for *Strong Verbs Spin, Lively Leads Spin,* and *Engaging Endings Spin*

Chapter
4

Onomatopoeia and Alliteration

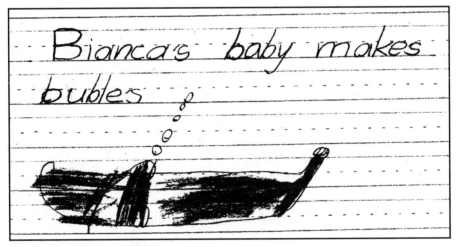

Figure 4.1 Bianca's Writing

Shirl's first graders enjoyed expanding their vocabularies as they experimented with vivid word choice. This chapter adds another level of enjoyment as students play with the sounds of language by using onomatopoeia and alliteration. As an example, Bianca took great pleasure in writing an alliterative sentence (see Figure 4.1).

When we introduce this VOICES category, we include the skills of onomatopoeia and alliteration. We use the sentence, "Splash! The duck dives deep into the pond" as a sample for both onomatopoeia and alliteration. We also use the picture of a duck in a pond as an accompanying illustration.

Onomatopoeia

Introductory Lessons

Shirl begins the first lesson by holding up the *O* poster and saying, "Today we're going to learn another thing good writers use. It's called onomatopoeia. Isn't that a funny word? *Onomatopoeia* means using sound words to give the reader a better picture." She then holds up the other posters and continues, "*O* stands for onomatopoeia. We'll also learn about alliteration in a few days. Here is a sentence that uses both onomatopoeia and alliteration, 'Splash! The duck dives deep into the pond.' What picture came into your brain when you heard those words?" As Shirl holds up the illustration, she says, "Here is a picture to remind us to use sound words. It's just like the picture you saw in your brain. The word *splash* is onomatopoeia because it is the sound that the duck made when it went into the pond. When you listen to stories and poems, we're going to be searching for sound words. When you find one, you can hold up your fingers to make an *O*. Here's our rhyme for onomatopoeia, 'Hold up an O when you hear a sound word.'" After saying the rhyming couplet (see Figure 4.2), students return to their current five-page books.

ONOMATOPOEIA

"Crash—bang—thump—screech—sizzle—tweet."
Onomatopoeia is a noisy treat.

Figure 4.2   Rhyming Couplet for Onomatopoeia

The second mini-lesson begins with a review of the previous day's work. After chanting the rhyming couplet several times, Shirl says, "Today we're going to make a chart on which we list all the onomatopoeia we hear. Let's sing the song 'The Wheels on the Bus,' and if you hear a sound word, make sure you hold up the *O* you make with your fingers. When we finish singing, we'll list the onomatopoeia that we hear." After singing, students begin the chart with the object and the sound from the song (e.g., horn—beep, wipers—swish). Shirl's lesson continues; she has the students sing "Are You Sleeping?" and adds the onomatopoeia *ding dong* to the class chart.

The next day's lesson reviews the rhyming couplet and the onomatopoeia chart; and Shirl states, "We're going to add onomatopoeia to a nursery rhyme. Let's use 'Little Miss Muffet' to add some sound words.

I'll do the first line. I think when Little Miss Muffet sat on her tuffet, it would make a squishing noise. So I'll write *squish* after the first line. What sound word could we use as Little Miss Muffet was eating her curds and whey?" The class brainstorms onomatopoeia for the rest of the nursery rhyme as follows:

> Little Miss Muffet sat on her tuffet (squish)
> Eating her curds and whey (slurp).
> Along came a spider who sat down beside her (plop),
> And frightened Miss Muffet away (screech!).

Shirl continues, "Let's add some of these words to our onomatopoeia chart. Can you think of any other sound words that we could add to our chart?" When the students have suggested other words, Shirl introduces the target practice. Using the sample sentence "The doorbell went ding dong," Shirl directs the students to write their own sentence with the pattern "The ___ went ___." Students complete the target practice activity (see Figure 4.3), then return to their current five-page books. Shirl ends this writing workshop session by having several students share their target practice sentence, then she warns, "Onomatopoeia is lots of fun to use in our writing. It gets the readers' attention and makes our piece more interesting. But if you use too many sound words, your writing will be too noisy!" Figure 4.4 shows the use of onomatopoeia in a student's independent writing.

Figure 4.3 Onomatopoeia Target Practice

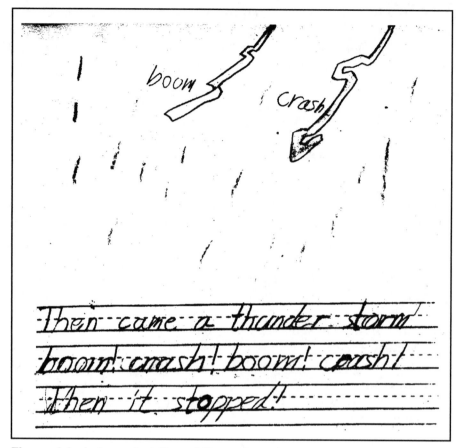

Figure 4.4   Independent Use of Onomatopoeia

After students have had these lessons on onomatopoeia, Shirl uses the skill to introduce another kind of lead. She begins, "When we were first learning about VOICES, we learned that authors experiment with different leads to hook their reader into reading more. We've already learned that an author can use action as an interesting lead. Authors sometimes use onomatopoeia as a lead, too. The onomatopoeia hooks readers so they keep on reading." Shirl has the nursery rhyme *Humpty Dumpty* on chart paper. She continues, "Let's use this nursery rhyme and change the lead by putting in a sound word. What might be the first word we could use as Humpty Dumpty fell off the wall?" The class experiments with words such as *Splat!, Plop!,* and *Whoosh!* On subsequent days, Shirl revisits some of her writing to add onomatopoeia as a lead, and she supports students as they revisit their leads to add a sound word.

Enrichment Activities

Children usually don't need much encouragement to use onomatopoeia in their writing – they love it! It's fun, however, to revisit this skill by locating onomatopoeia in literature and poetry. Figures 4.5 and 4.6 offer resources that Shirl uses to reinforce onomatopoeia throughout the year.

LITERATURE TITLES—ONOMATOPOEIA			
Title	**Author**	**Publisher**	**Copyright Date**
Why Mosquitoes Buzz in People's Ears	V. Aardema	Dial	1975
The Very Quiet Cricket	E. Carle	Philomel	1990
Mortimer	R. Munsch	Annick Press	1983
The Listening Walk	P. Showers	HarperCollins	1961
Cat Goes Fiddle-I-Fee	P. Galdone	Clarion	1985
Slop Goes the Soup	P. D. Edwards	Hyperion Books for Children	2001
Ding Dong Ding Dong	M. Palatini	Hyperion Books for Children	1999
The Happy Hedgehog Band	M. Waddell	Candlewick Press	1991
Crunch Munch	J. London	Harcourt	2001
Froggy Eats Out (and other books in this series)	J. London	Viking	2001
Feathers for Lunch	L. Ehlert	Scholastic	1990
Night Noises	M. Fox	Trumpet Club	1989
Barnyard Banter	D. Fleming	Henry Holt	1994
Click Clack Moo: Cows That Type	D. Cronin	Simon & Schuster	2000
City Sounds	J. Marzollo	Scholastic	1976
Good Night, Owl!	P. Hutchins	Aladdin	1972

Figure 4.5   Literature Titles for Teaching Onomatopoeia

POETRY TITLES—ONOMATOPOEIA		
Source: *The Random House Book of Poetry for Children* (Prelutsky, 1983)		
Title	**Author**	**Page Number**
"I'm Alone in the Evening"	Michael Rosen	142
"Fishes' Evening Song"	Dahlov Ipcar	78
"Our Washing Machine"	Patricia Hubbell	216
"We're Racing, Racing Down the Walk"	Phyllis McGinley	111
"A Thousand Hairy Savages"	Spike Milligan	150
"Toot! Toot!"	Anonymous	170
"The Tree Frog"	Jack Travers Moore	82
"Fernando"	Marci Ridlon	109
"March Wind"	Anonymous	41
"Barbershop"	Martin Gardner	113

Figure 4.6   Poetry Titles for Teaching Onomatopoeia

Shirl also uses onomatopoeia to reinforce the skill of patterning in math. Her students make patterns in many ways, such as AAB, circle circle square, clap clap snap, and so on. After learning about onomatopoeia in writing workshop, Shirl and her students use onomatopoetic sounds to form patterns (oink oink screech, for example). Sometimes they do this orally; and at other times, Shirl has her students write and illustrate a pattern for others to follow (see Figure 4.7).

Figure 4.7   Patterning With Onomatopoeia

To further practice onomatopoeia, Shirl uses the character cards found in appendix C for an activity called *Character Onomatopoeia*. A student selects a card from the character bag (described in chapter 3). The class then brainstorms a list of all the onomatopoetic sounds that could be associated with that character.

Once students have had lots of support as they've identified onomatopoeia, Shirl prepares a matching activity called *Onomatopoeia Match-Up* that she places in a literacy center so that students have an opportunity for independent practice. She writes an onomatopoetic word on one index card and the source of the sound on another. For example, if she writes *ding dong* on one card, she writes *doorbell* on the other. Once all the words are shuffled, students work alone or with a partner to match the pairs together (see appendix C for sample pairs). Shirl uses animal noises as the activity focus for one week and other onomatopoetic phrases for the next week. For the third week, she mixes up the two for a somewhat more difficult task.

Alliteration

Introductory Lessons

To begin the first mini-lesson on alliteration, Shirl says, "When we studied onomatopoeia, we learned that authors use sound words to help make their writing more interesting to their readers. Today, we're going to learn about another way that authors use sounds to make their writing more interesting. It's called *alliteration*. Sometimes a writer will repeat a sound in two or three different words. Our rhyme for alliteration has a sound that repeats. Listen as I read our alliteration rhyme." She reads the rhyming couplet (see Figure 4.8) and leads the class in a discussion of the alliteration within the rhyme. After chanting the rhyme several times, Shirl continues, "Today, we're going to write some alliteration using your names. We'll make tongue twisters with your names." Shirl asks a student to stand beside her. She guides students in thinking about action words and naming words that begin with the same sound as this student's name. The student then makes an alliterative sentence using his or her name (e.g., Sally slides in the sand, Bob bakes brownies, Jose honks the horn, Tom takes turns). Shirl guides the students in making several more alliterative sentences using their classmates' names. Finally, students get in knee-to-knee pairs (sitting together with their knees touching) and brainstorm other alliterative sentences using their partner's name. Students share some of their sentences with the class and then return to their current five-page books.

ALLITERATION

**Alliteration sounds so sweet.
It's a sound that does repeat.**

Figure 4.8   Rhyming Couplet for Alliteration

The second lesson begins with a review of the rhyming couplet and the previous day's mini-lesson. Shirl says, "Today we're going to write some alliteration using animals. We'll write the alliteration on this chart so you can remember them and use the alliteration in your own writing." She guides the class in a discussion of alliteration using an animal and its movement (e.g., the cat crawls, the dog digs, the monkey marches). As Shirl writes the alliteration on the chart, students act out each sentence.

The final mini-lesson on alliteration follows the same pattern as the previous day. During this lesson, however, students expand their use of alliteration by brainstorming ordinary objects and describing their movements, number, and other qualities. Shirl gives several examples that she then writes on the alliteration chart (e.g., one windy winter, two tired turtles, a little lazy lizard). Students then make contributions to the chart. Shirl removes the chart from view and gives the target practice assignment. Students write and illustrate an alliterative phrase (see Figure 4.9). For students who need additional help, Shirl confers with them in a small group, and they write an alliterative phrase together. Other students resume work on their five-page books.

Figure 4.9   Alliteration Target Practice

After students have participated in several lessons related to alliteration, Shirl relates these lessons to good leads. Her lesson begins, "We've studied good leads before. Who can remember the two ways to make a good lead that we've already studied?" Once students recall using action and onomatopoeia to write a lead, she displays the nursery rhyme *Little Bo Peep* and continues. "I'm going to experiment with a different lead for *Little Bo Peep*. I think I'll change Bo Peep's name to Little Lily Lou so her name makes an alliteration. So now my lead is 'Little Lily Lou has lost her sheep.' That's a pretty good alliteration. What if I changed the word *sheep* to *lambs?* That would be even better. How does this sound? 'Little Lily Lou has lost her lambs and doesn't know where to find them.' I like that alliteration, and I think it makes the lead more interesting." In subsequent days, Shirl revisits some of her writing to add an alliterative beginning, and she supports students as they revisit their leads to add alliteration.

Enrichment Activities

Locating alliterative phrases in literature and poetry is a wonderful enrichment opportunity. This activity helps keep children's ears "tuned" to the sounds of alliteration. Resources are found in Figures 4.10 and 4.11.

LITERATURE TITLES—ALLITERATION			
Title	**Author**	**Publisher**	**Copyright Date**
A Walk in the Rainforest	K. J. Pratt	Dawn	1992
The Magic Hat	M. Fox	Harcourt	2002
In the Small, Small Pond	D. Fleming	Scholastic	1993
Listen to the Rain	B. Martin, Jr. & J. Archambault	Henry Holt	1985
Gotcha	G. Jorgensen	Scholastic	1995
Jamberry	B. Degen	Scholastic	1983

Figure 4.10   Literature Titles for Teaching Alliteration

Reciting tongue twisters is a silly activity that Shirl's students love. We have included *Peter Piper* and *Betty Botter's Butter* in appendix C, and an Internet search will reveal several Web sites where other tongue twisters are available. Also found in appendix C are two Readers Theater scripts for fun tongue twister practice.

Shirl's students also enjoy selecting a cartoon character or action figure and composing an alliterative sentence. This can be done orally or in writing (e.g., Mickey Mouse makes many muffins or Superman sells slippery soap). The written sentences with accompanying illustrations make an attractive class book or bulletin board display.

POETRY TITLES—ALLITERATION Source: *The Random House Book of Poetry for Children* (Prelutsky, 1983)		
Title	**Author**	**Page Number**
"Spring"	Karla Kuskin	43
"Ants, Although Admirable, Are Awfully Aggravating"	Walter R. Brooks	74
"On the Ning Nang Nong"	Spike Mulligan	171
"The Yak"	Jack Prelutsky	197
"Sing Me a Song of Teapots and Trumpets"	N. M. Bodecker	193
"Night Comes…"	Beatrice Schenk de Regniers	33
"Spring"	Karla Kuskin	43
"Weather"	Anonymous	190
"The Tutor"	Carolyn Wells	190
"Clickbeetle"	Mary Ann Hoberman	193

Figure 4.11   Poetry Titles for Teaching Alliteration

A similar activity is called *Alliteration Spin.* Using the character cards and alliteration spinner, students create an alliterative sentence based upon the selection from the spinner. For instance, if the character is *astronaut* and the spinner shows *character's name,* then the sentence must contain alliteration based on an astronaut's name (e.g., Billy Bob worked at NASA.). If, however, the spinner landed on *place,* the alliteration would be based on where the astronaut was located (e.g., The astronaut flew to Mercury and Mars.).

Another fun activity is to make an *alliteration menu* together. Shirl and her students first study a sample menu to see that most are laid out in categories (e.g., appetizers, salads, entrees, desserts, and beverages). Next, they brainstorm different food items that could be found in each category. Finally each student selects a food item and composes (either orally or written) an alliterative phrase, like spicy spaghetti with munchy meatballs, fried fish, luscious lemonade, and crunchy carrot cake. An adaptation of this activity is to have students draw a picture of a food item, or cut one out from a newspaper or magazine, and then write an alliterative caption.

Preparation for Teaching

Resources for Lessons

- Posters:
  - –the large letter O
  - –the skills list
  - –the sample sentence
  - –the rhyming couplets for onomatopoeia and alliteration
- Traditional rhymes copied onto transparencies or chart paper:
  - –*Little Miss Muffet*
  - –*Humpty Dumpty*
  - –*Little Bo Peep*

Resources for Enrichment Activities

- Any book or poem listed in Figures 4.5, 4.6, 4.10, and 4.11
- Traditional rhymes copied onto transparencies or chart paper:
  - –*Peter Piper*
  - –*Betty Botter's Butter*
- Character Cards
- Alliteration spinner for *Alliteration Spin*
- *Onomatopoeia Match-Up* cards from appendix C copied onto index cards
- Alliteration Readers Theater scripts copied for each student
- Sample menus

Chapter

5

Interesting Dialogue and Interjections

Figure 5.1 Dianira's Writing

By mid-year, Shirl's students are writing with zeal. Their word choices are well considered, and they can easily locate onomatopoeia and alliteration in literature and poetry. Some students are beginning to use these craft elements in their independent writing. Now the students are ready to learn about interjections and dialogue. Both of these craft elements help students express their individuality and make their writing sound more like real "kid talk." In Figure 5.1, because of her use of an appropriate interjection, the reader knows that Dianira is distressed from her injured knee. Shirl highlights the interjection and displays Dianira's work on the VOICES bulletin board.

When we introduce this VOICES category, we use "'Wow! Look at that bug,' said Tom. Billy said, 'It's a huge cricket.'" as a sample for both dialogue and interjections. We also use the picture of two rabbits and a large cricket as an accompanying illustration.

Interesting Dialogue

Introductory Lessons

The introductory lesson for dialogue begins with Shirl saying, "Today we're going to be detectives. Detectives search for clues. As we read this big book, we're going to search for clues that tell us people are talking. We call conversation in books *dialogue.* When we write, we want to use interesting dialogue to get the attention of our readers. The words that show talking are surrounded by quotation marks." She introduces the sample sentence, icon, and rhyming couplet (see Figure 5.2), and the class chants the rhyme several times. Using a big book, Shirl shows examples of dialogue and explains the necessary punctuation. She uses *Mrs. Wishy Washy* by Joy Cowley (1980), but any big book with dialogue would be effective. She continues, "As I read this big book to you, I want you to be a detective and let me know when you hear some dialogue. You'll hear the characters talking. When you hear it, make our dialogue sign with your hands." Shirl shows them how to make a V with two fingers on each hand and wiggle them up and down to show quotation marks. When students identify the dialogue, she uses highlighter tape to draw attention to the quotation marks.

INTERESTING DIALOGUE

You use dialogue to show conversation.
Then you add special punctuation.

Figure 5.2   Rhyming Couplet for Interesting Dialogue

The second mini-lesson begins with a review of the rhyming couplet and the previous day's lesson. Shirl begins, "Today we're going to use the song *Old MacDonald* to help us think about the special punctuation that we use when we write dialogue. Let's practice this chant to help us remember. 'Comma, quotation, capital, period, quotation.'" She writes the code for this chant (, " *C* . ") on a sentence strip as they chant together.

Shirl explains that when we write dialogue, we first write who's talking, then put a comma, beginning quotation mark, capital letter, a period, and ending quotation mark. She also explains that sometimes the writer will use a question mark or exclamation point above the period. After reciting the chant several times, Shirl leads the class as they sing *Old MacDonald.* Then Shirl continues, "We're going to use this song to practice writing dialogue. We'll use this elbow macaroni and a frame sentence to practice the special punctuation used in dialogue. I'll show you what I mean. I think I'll write about the cow at Old MacDonald's farm. The cow says, 'Moo.' I'll draw a cow and use a speech bubble to show the cow saying, 'Moo.' Under my picture, I'll write my sentence and glue on this macaroni to show my quotation marks." Shirl demonstrates (see Figure 5.3) and then passes out paper and elbow macaroni for students to make their own picture and sentence based upon an animal from *Old MacDonald.*

Figure 5.3 Practice With Dialogue

Prior to the third mini-lesson, Shirl prepares sentence strips with dialogue from familiar fairy tales. She leaves the speaker unidentified. Sentences include the following: ___ said, "I'll huff, and I'll puff, and I'll blow your house down." ___ said, "Someone's been sleeping in my bed." ___ said, "Grandma, what big eyes you have." ___ said, "You can't catch me!" ___ said, "Fee, fi, fo, fum. I smell the blood of an Englishman." Shirl begins the lesson by reviewing the rhyming couplet and punctuation chant. She then says, "Today we're going to play a game called *Who Said It?* I'm going to read some dialogue to you, and you have to think about who said it. Are you ready?" She reads each sentence strip and allows students time to think about who the speaker might be. Once a student has guessed correctly, Shirl then writes the speaker's name to complete the sentence. After each sentence, she reviews the punctuation. Then Shirl assigns the target practice. She continues, "For target practice today, I want you to write a sentence using this frame: _____ said, _____. You can use dialogue you might want to say to a friend or dialogue you've heard from a favorite story. Remember to use the special punctuation: comma, quotation, capital, period, quotation. You might want to try a strong verb in place of *said*. Here's my target practice: Mrs. Hawes said, 'Do your best.'" Shirl writes her sample sentence, highlights the punctuation, and then dismisses students to do their target practice (see Figures 5.4 and 5.5) and resume work in their current five-page books. Figure 5.6 shows a student's independent use of dialogue within a five-page book.

Figure 5.4   Interesting Dialogue Target Practice

After teaching several mini-lessons on dialogue, Shirl relates these lessons to good leads. Her lesson begins, "We've studied good leads before. We know that we can use action, onomatopoeia, or alliteration to hook our reader." She displays the nursery rhyme *Little Miss Muffet* and continues. "I'm going to experiment with a different lead for *Little Miss Muffet*. I think I'll change the lead so that it uses dialogue. Dialogue is one kind of lead that writers use to hook their readers. Maybe the spider can be talking to Miss Muffet to begin the nursery rhyme. What would the spider say?" Students suggest phrases such as "Good morning," "Hello," and "I'm going to scare

Figure 5.5 More Target Practice

Figure 5.6 Independent Use of Dialogue

you." Then Shirl asks, "What would Miss Muffet say to the spider?" Students offer suggestions, and Shirl continues, "We've made a new lead for *Little Miss Muffet* using dialogue. We might say, 'Good morning,' said the spider. 'Get away from me!' said Miss Muffet as she sat on her tuffet eating her curds and whey. Now you know that when you begin a new piece, you can use action, onomatopoeia, alliteration, or dialogue to write an interesting lead to hook your readers." In subsequent days, Shirl revisits some of her writing to experiment with leads using dialogue, and she supports students as they revisit their leads to add dialogue.

Enrichment Activities

Shirl uses the macaroni activity described earlier for independent practice in a literacy center. She places blank paper, elbow macaroni, white glue, and her example (see Figure 5.3) in the center; and the students create other examples using speech bubbles and dialogue.

Dialogue can be located and studied in literature and poetry (see Figures 5.7 and 5.8). In addition, Shirl uses an activity she calls *Partner Dialogue.* After modeling the activity using a student as a partner, she pairs the students together. Two students get side-by-side, with two colors of marker and sharing a single piece of paper. They then have a conversation in writing. The first student uses one color to write an opening line, and the partner responds in writing with another color. (Second graders could add appropriate punctuation while completing this activity.) The "conversation" continues for about 10 minutes. As students complete this activity several times throughout the year, they get more and more competent with dialogue usage.

LITERATURE TITLES—INTERESTING DIALOGUE			
Title	**Author**	**Publisher**	**Copyright Date**
Hooray for Wodney Wat	H. Lester	Houghton Mifflin	1999
Ira Sleeps Over	B. Waber	Scholastic	1972
The Ghost-Eye Tree	B. Martin, Jr. & J. Archambault	Henry Holt	1985
Chrysanthemum	K. Henkes	Trumpet Club	1991
The Day Jimmy's Boa Ate the Wash	T. Noble	Scholastic	1980
Cook-a-Doodle-Doo	J. Stevens & S. S. Crummel	Harcourt Brace	1999

Figure 5.7   Literature Titles for Teaching Interesting Dialogue

POETRY TITLES—INTERESTING DIALOGUE		
Source: *The Random House Book of Poetry for Children* (Prelutsky, 1983)		
Title	**Author**	**Page Number**
"The Little Boy and the Old Man"	Shel Silverstein	161
"Tickle Rhyme"	Ian Serraillier	76
"Girls Can, Too"	Lee Bennett Hopkins	111
"Way Down South"	Anonymous	173

Figure 5.8 Poetry Titles for Teaching Interesting Dialogue

To complete the activity called *Character Dialogue,* a student selects one character card from the character bag. The class then brainstorms dialogue between two of the same characters (e.g., What would two astronauts say to each other?). An alternate activity is to have a student draw two cards and brainstorm dialogue between the two characters (e.g., What would a fireman say to a fox? What would a mom say to a boy? What would a king say to an astronaut?).

Students can take comic strips and translate those into dialogue. Shirl does this as a whole group lesson. They examine a comic strip, and then Shirl writes the dialogue on chart paper. Students suggest appropriate verbs to occasionally substitute for *said,* and they take turns punctuating sentences correctly. (After a few whole group sessions, second graders could do this activity independently.)

A similar though more advanced activity is to have students help convert a Readers Theater script into narrative text (A partial example is seen in Figure 5.9, and three scripts are located in appendix C.). Again

SCRIPT	NARRATIVE
	The Three Little Pigs
Narrator: Once upon a time, there were three little pigs.	Once upon a time, there were three little pigs. The first little pig wanted to build his own house, so he said, "I will build my house out of straw."
Pig 1: I will build my house out of straw.	
Pig 2: I think I'll use sticks.	The second little pig replied, "I think I'll use sticks."
Pig 3. I want to use bricks to make my house safe and strong.	The third little pig was the wise one. He warned, "I want to use bricks to make my house safe and strong."

Figure 5.9 Converting a Readers Theater Script Into Narrative

Shirl and her class do this together; second graders could attempt this activity with a partner.

Interjections

Introductory Lessons

Shirl's mini-lesson begins with an explanation of the meaning and function of interjections. She says, "Today we're going to learn about interjections. I'll bet you use interjections all the time and never knew it. An interjection is something you say when you're surprised, happy, or mad. It shows your strong feelings. Interjections are words like, 'Oh, no!' or 'Ouch!' or 'Whee!' or 'Ugh!' When you use an interjection, it makes your writing more exciting. To show our excitement, we usually put an exclamation mark after the interjection." Shirl introduces the rhyming couplet (see Figure 5.10), and the class chants it several times. Shirl continues, "Over the next few lessons, we'll be working to understand interjections and use them in our writing. Today we'll start a list of any interjections that we already know. Let's see if we can find an interjection in the nursery rhyme *Three Little Kittens.*" Shirl presents the nursery rhyme on chart paper or a transparency, and she leads her class in identifying the word *oh* as an interjection. The class begins a list of interjections, adding *oh* to the list. The students are then dismissed to continue their current five-page books.

INTERJECTIONS

"Wow!" cried the writer when he used an interjection.
"Making writing more exciting is a good suggestion."

Figure 5.10 Rhyming Couplet for Interjections

Prior to the next day's mini-lesson, Shirl writes a poem containing several interjections onto a chart paper. She uses "The Fourth" from Shel Silverstein's (1974) book *Where the Sidewalk Ends.* After reviewing the rhyming couplet, Shirl reads this poem and helps the students to identify and highlight the interjections. They add these words to the interjections list. Then she says, "Now I'm going to give you a situation, and we'll all brainstorm the interjections we'd use. For example, if I dropped a glass, I might say, 'Oops!' or 'Oh, no!' or 'Help!' I'll add those words to our

chart. As I say the situation, raise your hand if you can think of an interjection you'd use. Then I'll add those words to our list." Shirl gives situations such as:

> You skin your knee.
>
> You taste some food that's delicious.
>
> You taste some food that you don't like.
>
> You get a great present for your birthday.
>
> You see something amazing.
>
> You have a bad headache.
>
> You win a game.
>
> You go on a roller coaster.

As each interjection is offered, Shirl adds it to the chart, placing an exclamation mark after each one.

   The third lesson on interjections uses the book by Ruth Heller (1998)
entitled *Fantastic! Wow! and Unreal!: A Book About Interjections and Conjunctions.* Shirl first reviews the rhyming couplet and interjections list and
then reads the first half of Heller's book. As she reads, she leads the class
in a discussion of situations that might occur that would match some of
the interjections in the book. Because the book tells that interjections
change with the times, she shares some of the interjections that were
popular when she was a child (like "groovy," "holy cow," and "outasight").
Shirl then explains the target practice assignment. She tells them to use
an interjection from the chart to write and illustrate a sentence. Her
sample sentences include, "Oh no! I broke my mom's favorite vase." and
"Whee! I love to ride on a roller coaster." Shirl releases the students to
work on their target practice (see Figure 5.11) and their current five-
page books.

Figure 5.11 Interjections Target Practice

When the students have had several opportunities to learn about interjections, Shirl relates these mini-lessons to good leads. She begins, "We've studied good leads before. We know that we can use action, onomatopoeia, alliteration, or dialogue to hook our reader. Writers also can use an interjection as a lead to hook their readers." She displays the nursery rhyme *Wee Willie Winkie* on chart paper and reads it to the class. Shirl continues, "We know that Wee Willie Winkie was running through town in his nightgown. What interjection could we use at the beginning?" Students offer suggestions such as "Wow!" and "Oh my!" and "Look!" Shirl writes their suggestions on stick-on notes and places them at the beginning of the nursery rhyme. In subsequent days, Shirl revisits some of her writing to experiment with leads using interjections; and she supports students as they revisit their leads to add an interjection.

Enrichment Activities

To expand their repertoire of interjections, it's helpful to locate them in literature and poetry. (Figures 5.12 and 5.13 offer some resources.) In addition, *Interjections Charade* is one way that Shirl's students practice using interjections. To play, Shirl first prepares situation cards or asks her students to write their target practice sentences on sentence strips. (Situation cards might include: you fell and hurt your wrist, you're at your birthday party, or you just threw up.) She places these sentence strips in a bag or box, and she selects one student to be the actor. This student selects a sentence strip from the bag and acts it out without words. The rest of the students try and decide the situation and an appropriate interjection.

LITERATURE TITLES—INTERJECTIONS			
Title	**Author**	**Publisher**	**Copyright Date**
Oh My Baby Bear	A. Wood	Voyager Books	1990
Yo! Yes?	C. Raschka	Orchard Books	1993
That's Good! That's Bad!	M. Cuyler	Scholastic	1991
To Market, To Market	A. Miranda	Scholastic	1997

Figure 5.12   Literature Titles for Teaching Interjections

Another activity is called *Character Interjections*. A student selects a character card, and the class then brainstorms an interjection that the character might use, coupled with a statement that explains the reason the character would use that interjection. For example, if the character card

POETRY TITLES—INTERJECTIONS		
Source: *The Random House Book of Poetry for Children* (Prelutsky, 1983)		
Title	**Author**	**Page Number**
"In the Motel"	X. J. Kennedy	137
"Hey, Bug!"	Lilian Moore	72
"Pie Problem"	Shel Silverstein	148

Figure 5.13 Poetry Titles for Teaching Interjections

selected is *astronaut,* the statement might be, "All right! I blasted that alien to smithereens!"

Shirl uses a matching activity called *Interjections Match-Up* in a literacy center so students have some independent practice using interjections. To prepare this activity, she writes an interjection and a matching sentence on sentence strips (see appendix C). She then cuts them apart, separating the interjection from the sentence. In the literacy station, students match the pairs. Sometimes Shirl has students record several of the sentences that they've matched. For additional practice, students create their own matching set to add to the game.

Preparation for Teaching

Resources for Lessons

- Posters:
    - the large letter *I*
    - the skills list
    - the sample sentence
    - the rhyming couplets for interesting dialogue and interjections
- Traditional rhymes copied onto transparencies or chart paper:
    - *Little Miss Muffet*
    - *Three Little Kittens*
    - *Wee Willie Winkie*
- Suggested books:
    - *Mrs. Wishy Washy* (Cowley)
    - *Fantastic! Wow! and Unreal!: A Book About Interjections and Conjunctions* (Heller)

- Any poem from the ones suggested in Figure 5.13 copied onto chart paper or transparency
- Sentence strips:
    - _____ said, "I'll huff, and I'll puff, and I'll blow your house down."
    - _____ said, "Someone's been sleeping in my bed!"
    - _____ said, "Grandma, what big eyes you have!"
    - _____ said, "You can't catch me!"
    - _____ said, "Fee, fi, fo, fum. I smell the blood of an English-man."
- Elbow macaroni

Resources for Enrichment Activities

- Any book or poem from Figures 5.7, 5.8, 5.12, and 5.13
- Comic strips
- Readers Theater scripts from appendix C
- Character cards for *Character Dialogue* and *Character Interjections*
- Situation cards for *Interjections Charade*
- *Interjection Match-Up* from appendix C

Chapter

6   Comparison

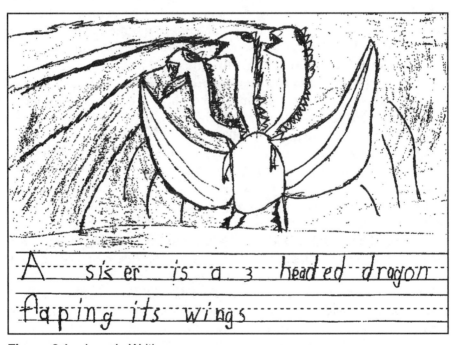

Figure 6.1 Jason's Writing

First graders understanding and using metaphors and personification? We were highly skeptical as we began discussing these craft elements. Surely these skills were too sophisticated for six and seven years old! As shown in Figure 6.1, in which Jason describes a pair of scissors, we underestimated our students' abilities to compare two things in complex ways.

When we introduce the VOICES category of comparison, we include the skills of simile, metaphor, and personification. We use the sentences "The rain played a sad song on my head. My hair felt like a wet mop." as a sample for the three kinds of comparison, and we use an accompanying illustration.

Simile

Introductory Lessons

To introduce comparisons, Shirl holds up the *C* poster and begins, "This *C* stands for *comparisons*. Good writers use comparison to show how two things are alike. They compare one thing to another thing. Here are the sentences that we will use to help us think about comparison. As I read our sentences, think about the picture you're getting in your brain. 'The rain played a sad song on my head. My hair felt like a wet mop.' What did you see in your brain?" The students talk about their mental images, and then Shirl holds up the accompanying illustration. She continues, "In these sentences, I compare the rain to a musician who plays a sad song. I also compare my hair to a wet mop because the rain makes my hair feel all limp and soggy. Today we'll study one kind of comparison called a *simile*. We are using a simile when we say that one thing is *like* another thing. Let's read our rhyming couplet and see what two things are being compared." Shirl reads the simile rhyme (see Figure 6.2), and the students chant it several times. Shirl guides the class in understanding that the rhyme compares writing to a strong bear. She asks, "When we say, 'A simile makes writing as strong as a bear,' we are comparing our writing and a bear. How are these two things alike?" After a discussion, Shirl continues, "That's right. Both our writing and a bear are strong. Our rhyming couplet uses a simile to help us compare strong writing to a strong bear. When we use a simile, we either use the words *like* or *as*. Now let's use the nursery rhyme *Twinkle, Twinkle, Little Star* to find another simile." Shirl reads the nursery rhyme and helps the students to identify the two things that are compared (a star and a diamond) and how they are alike (they both twinkle or shine). To end this mini-lesson, Shirl reads several sentences that she's written on sentence strips. She guides the students as they identify the two things being compared and how they are alike. Her sentences include the following:

> The rabbit is as soft as a pillow.
>
> The giant was as tall as a mountain.
>
> My dad's face felt like sandpaper.

Shirl also reads *Quick as a Cricket* by Audrey Wood (1982).

```
┌─────────────────────────────────────────────┐
│                                             │
│                  SIMILE                     │
│                                             │
│       When you use "like" or "as" to compare,│
│   A simile makes writing as strong as a bear!│
│                                             │
└─────────────────────────────────────────────┘
```

Figure 6.2 Rhyming Couplet for Simile

To begin the second lesson on similes, Shirl and her students recite the rhyming couplet. They then recite the first verse of *Mary Had a Little Lamb* to identify the two things being compared (lamb's fur and snow) and how they are the same (they are both white). Shirl says, "We are good at finding similes in other people's writing. Now we'll see if we can write some similes together. Today we'll use color words to compare two things. If I wanted to write about the red shirt I have on today, I could compare it to something else that's red. What are some things I could compare my shirt to?" The class brainstorms items that are red, and Shirl begins a simile chart by recording their ideas (e.g., as red as a sunburn, red like a tomato, as red as a Christmas ribbon). They then collaborate to create similes for color words to describe other items in the classroom, and Shirl records those on the chart, too. Examples include the following:

> The paper is as white as a marshmallow.
>
> His backpack is brown like chocolate.
>
> The door is as blue as the sky.
>
> The book is yellow like a lemon.

Students then return to their current five-page books.

The next mini-lesson begins with a review of strong verbs (see chapter 3). They chant the simile rhyming couplet, and then Shirl says, "When we studied strong verbs, we named many words we could use to show how something moves. Today, we'll use those strong verbs to make similes. We'll name a way to move, and then compare the movement to something else. Here's one to start with—I run like a ____. What could we compare the running to so that we finish the sentence?" The students brainstorm comparisons for Shirl's sentence and then create other similes with movements such as the following:

> I wiggle like a ____.
>
> I slither as fast as a ____.

I jump like a ____.

I spin like a ____.

As they chant each simile, the students act out the movement. Before sending the students to their seats, Shirl says, "When you are writing, you don't want to use similes too often. Maybe you could use one or two similes in each five-page book. If you use too many similes, your writing will sound very busy! Now we'll try our target practice. I want each of us to write and illustrate a simile. I think I'll write about being cold. I'll say, 'I am as cold as an ice cube.' Then I'll draw myself shivering." Shirl models the target practice with her simile and then has the students try the target practice assignment on their own (see Figures 6.3 and 6.4). In Figure 6.4, Arianne shows her understanding of the connection between the sentence's subject (herself) and its comparison (a mermaid) by connecting the two words with an arrow.

Figure 6.3 Simile Target Practice

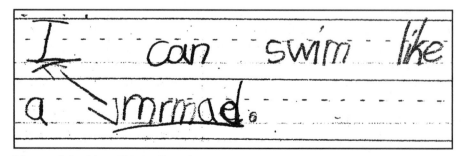

Figure 6.4 More Target Practice

Enrichment Activities

Shirl and her students revisit the use of simile at other times throughout the year. They make similes based on emotions, texture, size, taste, and temperature; and Shirl adds these comparisons to the class simile chart. They also locate simile in literature and poetry (see Figures 6.5 and 6.6).

LITERATURE TITLES—SIMILE			
Title	Author	Publisher	Copyright Date
Quick as a Cricket	A. Wood	Child's Play	1982
Owl Moon	J. Yolen	Philomen Books	1987
My Dad	A. Browne	Farrar Straus Giroux	2000
The Tale of Custard the Dragon	O. Nash	Little, Brown	1936/1995

Figure 6.5   Literature Titles for Teaching Simile

POETRY TITLES—SIMILE		
Source: *The Random House Book of Poetry for Children* (Prelutsky, 1983)		
Title	Author	Page Number
"Flint"	Christina Rossetti	23
"Easter"	Joyce Kilmer	42
"Spring"	Karla Kuskin	42
"Oliphaunt"	J. R. R. Tolkein	59
"Zebra"	Judith Thurman	93
"A Dragonfly"	Eleanor Farjeon	75

Figure 6.6   Poetry Titles for Teaching Simile

The class revisits *Quick as a Cricket* to expand their repertoire of simile. Shirl selects one simile within the text, and the class brainstorms other similar comparisons. For example, for the simile "quick as a cricket," the students may offer "quick as a racecar," or rabbit, cheetah, rocket, and so on. Shirl encourages them to consider other things besides animals. Different similes from the text are discussed on other days. Shirl makes a chart for each brainstorming session and displays it in the classroom.

An entertaining and educational activity to reinforce similes is to have students compose *Simile Riddles*. Shirl gives each student a white piece of construction paper that is then folded in half like a greeting card. Students write a simile riddle on the front (for example, What is as cold as ice? What is red like a tomato?), and then they illustrate and write the answer in the middle (a popsicle, Rudolph's nose). Once all students have completed their riddles, the cards are placed in a literacy center for students to enjoy. At another time, Shirl puts blank cards in a writing center, and students make additional riddle cards to contribute to the class collection.

Metaphor

Introductory Lessons

To begin the first mini-lesson on metaphor, Shirl introduces the rhyming couplet (see Figure 6.7). After the class chants it several times, Shirl continues, "When we use a metaphor, we compare two things to see how they are alike, just as we did when we wrote similes. But metaphors are trickier because they don't use *like* or *as* to compare. In our rhyming couplet, we said that a metaphor is a window into a book. Of course, we know that a metaphor isn't really a window. We compare a metaphor to a window because they both give us a look. A window helps us to look into a building, and a metaphor helps us to look at a comparison. If I say, 'My mom is a dragon when she's mad,' I don't mean that she's a real dragon. I'm comparing my mom to a dragon because they're both ferocious when they're mad! Now let's see if we can find the metaphor in a poem. Remember that a metaphor makes a comparison." Any poem with an obvious metaphor is appropriate for use in this lesson. Shirl reads the poem "The Toaster" by William Jay Smith (Prelutsky, 1983). In this poem, Smith compares a toaster to "a silver-scaled dragon with jaws flaming red." Shirl and her students discuss what is being compared (a toaster and a dragon) and how they are alike (they both use fire). Next, Shirl holds up a stapler and continues, "We've seen how William Jay Smith compares a toaster to a dragon. He used a metaphor to compare. Now let's try to use this stapler to write a metaphor. How is this stapler like an animal? What animal could we use to describe a stapler? What is the animal stapler doing to the paper?" As the students answer her questions, Shirl guides the students in brainstorming several examples of metaphor related to the stapler. Examples include the following:

> A stapler is a greedy alligator snapping at a pile of papers.
>
> A stapler is a Tyrannosaurus chomping on two papers.
>
> A stapler is a hungry wolf biting the paper's corner.

Shirl records the suggestions on chart paper, and then the students continue working on their current five-page books.

METAPHOR

A metaphor is a window into your book.
When you compare two things, you get a better look.

Figure 6.7 Rhyming Couplet for Metaphor

The second mini-lesson begins with a review of the metaphor rhyming couplet. Shirl next asks the students to listen as she reads the nursery rhyme *Mary, Mary, Quite Contrary.* She says, "This rhyme says that Mary's garden had silver bells and pretty maidens in it. Maidens are girls. Would bells and girls really be growing in a garden? No! What really grows in gardens? Yes, the rhyme is comparing the flowers in Mary's garden to bells and girls." Shirl shows several pictures of flowers (from a seed catalog or downloaded from the Internet). The students discuss the similarities between flowers and silver bells, and between flowers and pretty girls all in a row. Shirl then holds up a pencil and asks, "What do you think about when you see this pencil? Does it remind you of anything special? Think about the pencil's color, its shape, and how it moves. When we write a metaphor about this pencil, we want to relate this pencil to what it does—it writes words or draws pictures." The students discuss possible comparisons, and Shirl helps them to hone their suggestions into metaphorical statements, which she adds to the chart paper from the previous day. Each example includes the pencil, the comparison, and a relationship to writing or drawing. Examples include the following:

> A pencil is a yellow bus full of pictures.
>
> A pencil is a ballerina dancing across the paper.
>
> A pencil is a rocket shooting words into space.

The third mini-lesson on metaphor is an adaptation from the book *Teeth, Wiggly as Earthquakes* by Judith Tannenbaum (2000). After reviewing the rhyming couplet, Shirl begins by stating, "Today we'll write some metaphors by comparing ourselves to our favorite things. What are some things that you like a lot?" She writes these things on the board (e.g., animals, cartoon characters, toys, sports equipment, games, or places). She continues, "To write a metaphor, I'm going to think about something that's a favorite of mine. I will compare myself to something I like.

I really like to visit the ocean, so I could write, 'I am a wild wave crashing against the shore.' That sentence compares me to the ocean's wave. You know that I love hedgehogs, so I could write, 'I am a prickly hedgehog curled up into a sleepy ball.' What am I comparing in that sentence?" After discussion, Shirl says, "I didn't just write, 'I'm a hedgehog.' I told *how* I was like a hedgehog. Now you're going to get knee-to-knee and try to make some metaphors with each other. You'll think about things you like, just as I did, and compare each other to those things. Remember to tell what you are doing in your metaphor!" Shirl moves from pair to pair, listening to their metaphors and supporting the partners who need help. After approximately 5 minutes have passed, students write and illustrate a metaphor for target practice and then return to their current five-page books. Figure 6.8 shows one example of metaphor writing from Shirl's class.

Figure 6.8   Metaphor Usage

Enrichment Activities

Metaphor is abstract and requires lots of discussion so that most students can recognize and attempt to use them in their writing. Therefore, drawing attention to metaphor in books and poems is helpful. Figures 6.9 and 6.10 offer a few resources; we've found that it's easier to use poetry. In addition, whole texts are sometimes metaphorical. For example, *Mrs. Spitzer's Garden* (Pattou, 2001) is about a lady and her garden, but it's a metaphor for teaching. With texts such as this one, Shirl models how she's interpreted the abstract meaning of the book.

LITERATURE TITLES—METAPHOR			
Title	**Author**	**Publisher**	**Copyright Date**
Mrs. Spitzer's Garden	E. Pattou	Harcourt	2001

Figure 6.9   Literature Titles for Teaching Metaphor

POETRY TITLES—METAPHOR Source: *The Random House Book of Poetry for Children* (Prelutsky, 1983)		
Title	**Author**	**Page Number**
"Dandelion"	Hilda Conkling	25
"The Night Is a Big Black Cat"	G. Orr Clark	33
"The Toaster"	William Jay Smith	217

Figure 6.10   Poetry Titles for Teaching Metaphor

Personification

Introductory Lessons

Shirl introduces the skill of personification by saying, "Today we're going to learn one more ways to write a comparison. It's called *personification.* As I write the word on the board, you can see the word *person* hidden at the beginning. That will help you to remember what personification is. Personification allows a nonhuman character to act like a person. Let's learn our rhyme about personification." Shirl reads the rhyming couplet (see Figure 6.11), and the class chants it several times. She continues, "In this rhyme, the sun is acting like a human because it is smiling. In our comparison sentence, 'The rain played a sad song on my head,' the rain is acting like a human because it is playing a sad song. Whenever a nonhuman character acts like a person, it's called *personification.* Now I'll read two nursery rhymes, and I want you to listen to see if you can identify the characters that act like humans." She reads *Hey Diddle Diddle* and *Three Little Kittens,* and the students discuss the personification within the two rhymes. They chant the rhyming couplet again and then return to their current five-page books.

To prepare for the second lesson on personification, Shirl writes the poem "April Rain Song" by Langston Hughes on chart paper (from *The Random House Book of Poetry for Children* [Prelutsky, 1983]). After the class chants the rhyming couplet, Shirl asks the students to identify how the rain acts like a human (kissing and singing a lullaby). She then says,

```
┌─────────────────────────────────────────────────┐
│                                                 │
│                 PERSONIFICATION                 │
│                                                 │
│     "The sun smiles down on me" is personification. │
│       To make animals and things act like people, │
│                use your imagination.            │
│                                                 │
└─────────────────────────────────────────────────┘
```

Figure 6.11   Rhyming Couplet for Personification

"Today we're going to write some sentences with personification. To write personification, we need to think about an object that will act like a human. Let's list some things that only people can do." The students brainstorm actions done by people, and Shirl writes their ideas on the board. Then she says, "Now we're going to try to think about an object doing something from this list. I'll try one. To write personification, I need to think about an object, an action word, and a human outcome—something only a human can do. We have the word *sings* on our list. I'll write about a caterpillar singing. 'A caterpillar sings a munching song as it crawls along the leaf.' Can a caterpillar really sing a song? No! I've used personification to make my caterpillar do an action that only a human can really do. Let's try some together." Shirl guides her students as they create expanded sentences with an object, an action word, and a human outcome. Examples include the following:

> This rock wonders how it got to be so small.
>
> A cloud paints castles in the sky.
>
> My pencil hopes that I will sharpen it soon.
>
> The book wants me to read it.

The next mini-lesson on personification begins with a review of the rhyming couplet. Shirl says to her students, "Now we'll sing *I'm a Little Teapot.* I want you to try to find the personification in this song. Raise you hand if you hear the teapot acting like a human." The students identify the personification (the teapot shouting, "Come tip me over and pour me out."). Shirl continues, "Today we'll write some personification that uses dialogue. I'll write our dialogue on this chart. Remember that when we write dialogue, we show that our character says something. It has special punctuation: comma, quotation, capital, period, quotation. To do this activity, we'll think of what an object might say if it were human. What would a spoon say?" Students offer suggestions, and Shirl writes them on the chart. Examples include the following:

> The spoon screamed, "Your ice cream is melting all over me!"

The spoon sighed, "I can't wait to dive into the bowl of ice cream."

The spoon screeched, "This soup is too hot!"

Shirl and her students consider other dialogue for inanimate objects (What would a pencil say? A vacuum cleaner? A mirror? A car? A flower?). After brainstorming several ideas for each object, Shirl assigns the target practice. Students write and illustrate a sentence with dialogue in which an object talks like a human. Though many students need lots of support to understand and use personification, Figures 6.12 and 6.13 show two first graders' effective use of personification.

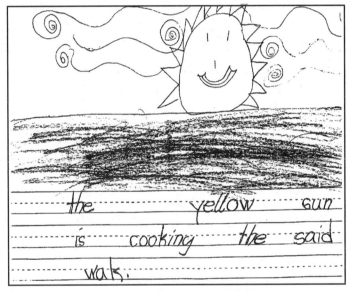

Figure 6.12 Personification Target Practice—
"The yellow sun is cooking the sidewalk."

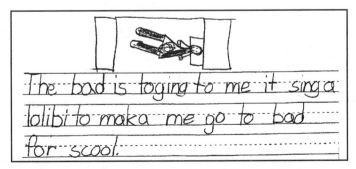

Figure 6.13 Independent Use of Personification—
*"The bed is talking to me. It sings
a lullaby to make me go to bed for school."*

Enrichment Activities

As with metaphor, personification is difficult for many primary children. Shirl uses literature and poetry to draw the students' attention to a writer's use of effective personification (see Figures 6.14 and 6.15 for suggestions).

LITERATURE TITLES—PERSONIFICATION			
Title	Author	Publisher	Copyright Date
Alphabet Adventures	A. Wood	Blue Sky Press	2001
Babushka's Doll	P. Polacco	Aladdin	1990
Mirandy and Brother Wind	P. McKissack	Trumpet Club	1988
Corduroy	D. Freeman	Scholastic	1968

Figure 6.14   Literature Titles for Teaching Personification

POETRY TITLES—PERSONIFICATION Source: *The Random House Book of Poetry for Children* (Prelutsky, 1983)		
Title	Author	Page Number
"The March Wind"	Anonymous	41
"The Wind"	James Reeves	26
"Until I Saw the Sea"	Lilian Moore	29
"The Moon's the North Wind's Cooky"	Vachel Lindsay	32
"Easter"	Joyce Kilmer	42
"Crickets"	Valerie Worth	73
"Sunrise"	Frank Asch	93
"Fog"	Carl Sandburg	96
"April Rain Song"	Langston Hughes	97
"City"	Langston Hughes	98
"Foghorns"	Lilian Moore	98

Figure 6.15   Poetry Titles for Teaching Personification

After Shirl has introduced simile, metaphor, and personification, she relates these three forms of comparison to good leads. She begins, "We've talked a lot about good leads before. We know that we can use action, onomatopoeia, alliteration, dialogue, or interjection to hook our reader.

Writers also use comparison to hook their readers. They might use a simile, metaphor, or personification as a lead." She displays the nursery rhyme *There Was an Old Woman Who Lived in a Shoe* on chart paper and reads it to the class. Shirl continues, "Let's see if we can experiment with the beginning of this nursery rhyme by using a comparison to tell how old the lady was. Maybe we could say, 'There was a woman as old as a dinosaur.' What else can you think of that's really old that we could compare the old woman to?" The students offer suggestions, such as "old as the earth," or "old as a mummy." In subsequent days, Shirl revisits some of her writing to experiment with leads using a comparison, and she supports students as they revisit their leads to add a simile, metaphor, or personification.

Another activity to reinforce the three types of comparison is called *Comparisons Spin*. For this activity, Shirl copies, laminates, and cuts out the object cards found in appendix C. She also prepares the comparison spinner. A student selects an object card and spins the spinner. The class then brainstorms possible comparisons using the object card as the subject of a sentence. Examples for the object *book* include the following:

- Simile—A book is like a magic time machine.

- Metaphor—A book is a door to new places.

- Personification—The book grabbed me by the hand and took me to visit a strange castle.

Preparation for Teaching

Resources for Lessons

- Posters:
  - –the large letter *C*
  - –the skills list
  - –the sample sentence
  - –the rhyming couplets for similes, metaphors, and personification

- Traditional rhymes copied onto transparencies or chart paper:
  - –*Twinkle, Twinkle, Little Star*
  - –*Mary Had a Little Lamb*
  - –*Mary, Mary, Quite Contrary*
  - –*Hey Diddle Diddle*
  - –*Three Little Kittens*
  - –*I'm a Little Teapot*

- Suggested book: *Quick as a Cricket* (Wood)
- The poem "April Rain Song" copied onto chart paper or transparency
- Sentence strips:
  - –The rabbit is as soft as a pillow.
  - –The giant was as tall as a mountain.
  - –My dad's face felt like sandpaper.

Resources for Enrichment Activities

- Any book or poem from Figures 6.5, 6.6, 6.9, 6.10, 6.14, and 6.15
- Suggested book: *Mrs. Spitzer's Garden* (Pattou)
- Traditional rhyme copied onto transparencies or chart paper:
  - –*There Was an Old Woman Who Lived in a Shoe*
- Object cards and comparison spinner from appendix C for *Comparisons Spin*

Chapter

7   Expand One Idea

Figure 7.1   Irene's Writing

Irene recently learned about using transition words related to time. Her enthusiasm for applying her new knowledge is seen in Figure 7.1 where she eagerly wrote three sentences using time transition words. In this chapter, we'll describe how Shirl helped her students narrow a topic, expand it, use transition words, and write to evoke emotions in their readers.

When we introduce this VOICES category we use the sentences "Suddenly, a door creaked open. Out slithered an enormous dragon." as a sample for this category. We also use an accompanying illustration. In addition, we use a balloon throughout these lessons as a metaphor for expansion. We tell the students that boring writing is like a balloon that hasn't been blown up. Just like a balloon, writing is better when it's expanded.

Narrow the Topic and Expand One Idea

Introductory Lessons

Shirl begins this mini-lesson near the overhead projector as she first introduces the *E* and the skills posters, sample sentence, and icon. She then tells her students, "I'm going to write about my weekend." She begins to write on a transparency, "'I went to Dallas this weekend. I went to a teachers' meeting. I went with my friend Debbie. We got lost on our way there. Debbie's mother made cookies for us to take with us. I learned a lot at the meeting. Then we drove back to Houston." Shirl stops and rereads, then says, "You know, that sounds kind of boring. It seems more like a list and it doesn't have many details. I have a lot of little stories that I could write that tell about my trip to Dallas. I think I'll try to narrow my topic. When we narrow a topic, we pick one small piece of a big idea. I could write about staying with Debbie's mom on our trip, or I could write about talking with Debbie on our drive to Dallas. I could write about what I learned at the teachers' meeting. I think I've decided to narrow my topic and write about one part of my trip—getting lost on the way to the meeting." Shirl introduces the rhyming couplet (see Figure 7.2) by acting it out. She begins by spreading her arms apart and bringing them close together as she says, "Narrow your topic." When she says, "Write about one thing," she holds up one finger. Shirl wags her finger back and

---

NARROW THE TOPIC

Narrow your topic. Write about one thing.
You don't have to tell about everything.

Figure 7.2 Rhyming Couplet for Narrowing the Topic

forth as she continues, "You don't have to tell about everything." As she says the final word, Shirl again spreads her arms apart. Her students act out the rhyming couplet as they chant it.

Shirl then displays the nursery rhyme *Jack and Jill*. She reads it and then says, "This nursery rhyme doesn't tell all about Jack and Jill's day. It doesn't say what they had for breakfast, what they did at school, or what chores they did at home. The writer of this nursery rhyme narrowed the topic and wrote about only one thing that Jack and Jill did. As we write, we want to think about narrowing our topics, too." They review the rhyming couplet, and then the students continue on their current five-page books.

This mini-lesson on expanding the topic immediately follows the lesson on narrowing the topic. Shirl wants to help her students understand that once a writer has narrowed the topic, one idea needs to be expanded to help readers understand the topic better. Shirl begins by reviewing the previous day's lesson. "We've learned that writers often narrow their topic instead of writing about everything that happened. I decided to write about my trip to Dallas, but I decided that it would be more interesting if I just wrote about a small moment instead of the whole trip. I'm going to begin my five-page book now about how Debbie and I got lost on our way to the teachers' meeting. Before I write, though, I want to think about my ideas. I can't just say, 'Debbie and I got lost on our way to a meeting.' That's not enough information for my readers! I want to give enough useful information so the reader will have a clear idea of what's happening in my piece. I have a rhyme that will help us know how to give useful information. The rhyme is called 'Expand One Idea.' *Expand* means to make bigger. When I blow up a balloon, I expand it. When I write, I want to take a small idea and make it bigger." Shirl introduces the rhyming couplet (see Figure 7.3), and the class chants it several times.

EXPAND ONE IDEA

When you expand one idea with useful information—
like "who, what, where, when, how, and why"—
you'll improve communication.

Figure 7.3 Rhyming Couplet for Expand One Idea

On chart paper, Shirl lists "who, what, where, when, how, why." She says, "These words from our rhyme will help me to think about expanding my idea. I'll fill in the chart with useful information that will help me write my piece." (Shirl's chart is shown in Figure 7.4.) After she completes the chart, she continues, "Now I've got some useful information that will help me to expand one idea." As usual, the students return to their current five-page books once this lesson is completed.

Who:	Debbie and I
What:	got lost on our way to a teachers' meeting
Where:	on the freeway in downtown Dallas
When:	early one morning when traffic was very heavy
How:	We thought we knew where we were going.
Why:	We didn't look at a map or read the signs carefully.

Figure 7.4 Expanding One Idea

The next day's mini-lesson begins with Shirl displaying the children's book *The Paperboy* (Pilkey, 1996). (Any book about a small moment would be appropriate.) She says, "Let's look at how a published author has narrowed his topic and expanded on one idea. This book is about a boy who delivers papers. The author could have written about the boy's whole day. Instead, the author has narrowed the topic. The book is only about one small moment of the boy's day. The idea is expanded so that the reader learns useful information about the boy's morning paper deliveries." After Shirl reads the book, they discuss the author's craft and read the rhyming couplets related to narrowing the topic and expanding one idea. The students continue working on their five-page books.

Target practice is done after the class has taken a field trip to the zoo. (Any interesting shared experience is appropriate for this lesson.) Shirl models how to make a time line of the events that she remembers from their field trip. Students then make their own time lines based on their personal memories of the trip. Shirl encourages students to select the most memorable event from their time lines so that they can expand this idea orally. She pairs students together for knee-to-knee discussions to recall details of who, what, where, when, how, and why in order to expand their idea. Shirl suggests that students pretend to be watching a video of that moment in their head, and they should tell their partner everything that is happening. To monitor the target practice, Shirl moves from group to group, assessing and guiding their discussions.

Enrichment Activities

The enrichment activity described here can be used throughout the remainder of the year. Every once in a while, Shirl either models or guides her class as they make time lines of a recent occurrence. After the time lines have been constructed, the students discuss and select one item on their time line that would make an interesting topic for writing. Shirl doesn't insist that students write about the topic; she just wants to create discussion around narrowing the topic.

Shirl uses the character cards to teach an activity called *Action Expansion*. A student selects a character card from the character bag. Next, the class creates a time line of all the activities the character might do. They decide on one of the character's activities to expand on and then use question words to expand the idea. For example, if the character card selected is *queen,* the students might use question words as follows:

Who: the queen

What: had a fight with the wizard

Where: in the prince's bedroom

When: one night

How: in an angry voice

Why: the wizard was trying to turn the prince into a frog

An extension of this activity is to have students draw two character cards and create a scenario that occurs between the two.

The use of literature presents the perfect format to discuss how authors narrow a topic and expand it to form a book (see Figure 7.5). In addition, many poems capture a small moment (see Figure 7.6). Throughout the remainder of the school year, Shirl uses both of these resources to review the skills of narrowing the topic and expanding one idea.

LITERATURE TITLES—NARROWING THE TOPIC & EXPANDING ONE IDEA			
Title	Author	Publisher	Copyright Date
Swish!	B. Martin, Jr. & J. Archambault	Henry Holt	1997
The Paperboy	D. Pilkey	Scholastic	1996
Lost	P. B. Johnson & C. Lewis	Scholastic	1996

Figure 7.5   Literature Titles for Teaching Narrowing the Topic and Expanding One Idea

POETRY TITLES—NARROWING THE TOPIC & EXPANDING ONE IDEA Source: *The Random House Book of Poetry for Children* (Prelutsky, 1983)		
Title	**Author**	**Page Number**
"Cat"	Mary Britton Miller	68
"Every Time I Climb a Tree"	David McCord	119
"On Mother's Day"	Aileen Fisher	43
"Sunning"	James S. Tippett	66
"A Dragonfly"	Eleanor Farjeon	75
"The Hen"	Lord Alfred Douglas	85
"Open Hydrant"	Marci Ridlon	96
"Fernando"	Marci Ridlon	109
"We're Racing, Racing Down the Walk"	Phyllis McGinley	111
"Soap"	Martin Gardner	138
"Accidentally"	Maxine W. Kumin	150
"Did You Ever Go Fishing?"	Anonymous	180
"Foul Shot"	Edwin A. Hoey	220

Figure 7.6   Poetry Titles for Teaching Narrowing the Topic and Expanding One Idea

Transition Words

Introductory Lessons

Shirl's next mini-lesson involves writing a draft of her "Losing the Way" piece that she's discussed before. She begins, "I know that I want to write about my trip to Dallas when Debbie and I lost our way, and I've expanded my idea to give useful information to my readers. Now I'm going to start my piece on this transparency before I begin my five-page book. As I write, listen to see if you can give me some advice for making my piece better." Shirl writes, "Debbie and I were driving to the meeting in Dallas. And then we noticed that we were lost. And then we said, 'Oh, no! Where are we?' And then we looked around and noticed that we were driving away from our meeting place. And then we had to turn around. And then we drove through the busy streets. And then we were still lost. And then we got out a map and found our way to our meeting."

Shirl asks her students, "Do you have any advice for making my piece better?" Shirl accepts ideas until someone says that *and then* has been used too often. She continues, "That's right. I keep writing, 'and then . . . and then . . . and then.' How boring! My readers would probably fall asleep! I need to use other transition words. *Transition words* are words we can use in place of *and then*, like *next, first,* or *suddenly.* Transition words help a reader to move smoothly from one idea to another. They tell when or where something happened. I have a rhyme that will help us to learn about transition words." Shirl introduces the rhyming couplet (see Figure 7.7), and the class chants it several times. She then says, "Tomorrow we'll begin a list of words we can use in place of *and then* so our readers won't be snoring!"

TRANSITION WORDS

"And then," "and then," "and then," "and then" gets
a little boring. Use other transition words
so your readers won't be snoring!

Figure 7.7 Rhyming Couplet for Transition Words

The next day, the class reviews the rhyming couplet for transition words. Then Shirl says, "When we use transition words, we tell either when something happened or where something happened. Today we're going to learn about transition words that tell us about time. We call them *time transition words.* These words tell us when something happened. I've started a chart with some time words that we can use as we write. We might use words like *today, yesterday, on Saturday,* or *first.* Listen as I read a couple of nursery rhymes, and give me a thumbs up when you hear words that tell when something happened." Shirl reads several nursery rhymes with transition words related to time (e.g., *Hickory Dickory Dock, Old Mother Hubbard, Wee Willie Winkie*), and then the class brainstorms other time transition words to add to the chart. (See Figure 7.8 for some examples of time transition words.) For target practice, Shirl has her students write and illustrate a sentence that uses a time transition word. Her example is "Yesterday we went to the beach." Figure 7.9 illustrates a student's target practice with time transition words.

Shirl begins the next mini-lesson reviewing the rhyming couplet and the chart with time transition words. She continues, "We know some transition words that tell us when something happened, and today we're going to learn about transition words that tell us where something happened. These are called *location transition words* because they tell us where something is located. Location words are usually found at the end of a sentence." As in

Time Transition Words	Location Transition Words
about	above
after	across
afterward	against
as soon as	along
at	among
before	around
during	behind
first	below
second	beneath
third	beside
until	between
meanwhile	beyond
immediately	by
finally	in back of
today	in front of
tomorrow	inside
on (date or day of week)	into
last (day of week or month)	near
next week	off
yesterday	onto
soon	on bottom of
suddenly	on top of
later	outside
when	over
in (month)	throughout
	to the left
	to the right
	under

Figure 7.8   Transition Words Chart

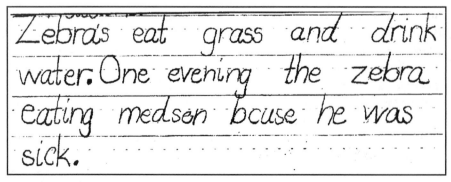

Figure 7.9   Use of Time Transition Words

the lesson on time transition words, Shirl introduces several location words on a chart, reads some nursery rhymes with location words (e.g., *Jack and Jill, Little Miss Muffet, Humpty Dumpty*), and then guides the class as they create a chart with location transition words. (See Figure 7.8 for some location transition words.) She uses a puppet to act out some of the words to help students visualize the various locations. Before returning to their current five-page books, the class completes a target practice by writing and illustrating a sentence that uses a location transition word (see Figure 7.10). Shirl's example is "I saw a little mouse under the table."

Figure 7.10 Use of Location Transition Words

Enrichment Activities

Transition words can be located and discussed using literature and poetry. Suggested books and poems are found in Figures 7.11 and 7.12.

LITERATURE TITLES—TRANSITION WORDS			
Title	**Author**	**Publisher**	**Copyright Date**
Olivia Saves the Circus	I. Falconer	Antheneum Books for Young Readers	2001
The Very Hungry Caterpillar	E. Carle	Scholastic	1969
Pig Pig and the Magic Photo Album	D. McPhail	E. P. Dutton	1986
Each Peach Pear Plum	J. & A. Ahlberg	Puffin	1978
Wheel Away!	D. Dodds	Scholastic	1989

Figure 7.11 Literature Titles for Teaching Transition Words

POETRY TITLES—TRANSITION WORDS			
Source: *The Random House Book of Poetry for Children* (Prelutsky, 1983)			
Type of Transition Word	**Title**	**Author**	**Page Number**
Time	"Windy Nights"	Robert Louis Stevenson	27
	"Crickets"	Valerie Worth	73
	"That May Morning"	Leland B. Jacobs	93
	"City"	Langston Hughes	98
	"Eat-It-All Elaine"	Kaye Starbird	108
	"Basketball Star"	Karama Fufuka	123
	"The Wrong Start"	Marchette Chute	132
	"The Worm"	Ralph Bergengren	151
	"One Misty, Moisty Morning"	Anonymous	157
	"Our Washing Machine"	Patricia Hubbell	216
	"Keep a Poem in Your Pocket"	Beatrice Schenk de Regiers	226
Location	"Rain Clouds"	Elizabeth-Ellen Long	30
	"Check"	James Stephens	32
	"Night"	Mary Ann Hoberman	33
	"Cats"	Eleanor Farjeon	68
	"Samuel"	Bobbi Katz	81
	"The Blackbird"	Hubert Wolfe	83
	"Zebra"	Judith Thurman	93
	"The People"	Elizabeth Madox Roberts	93
	"Sing a Song of People"	Lois Lenski	95
	"April Rain Song"	Langston Hughes	97
	"Bubble Gum"	Nina Payne	106
	"We're Racing, Racing Down the Walk"	Phyllis McGinley	111
	"When I Was Lost"	Dorothy Aldis	120
	"This is Just to Say"	William Carlos Williams	146
	"Daddy Fell in the Pond"	Alfred Noyes	156
	"What's That?"	Florence Parry Heide	201
	"Driving to the Beach"	Joanna Cole	217

Figure 7.12   Poetry Titles for Teaching Transition Words

Shirl uses two activities to reinforce transition words. Either activity can be done orally or in writing. One activity is called *Transition Word Riddles*. Shirl asks her students to compose riddles related to time or location. The riddle questions can be based upon realistic events (When do we go to P.E.?) or fanciful (When did Dorothy land in Oz?). She expects the answer to be given in a complete sentence (e.g., We go to P.E. at 10:30 on Tuesdays. Dorothy landed in Oz after the tornado.).

Another enrichment activity is a class favorite. Shirl calls it *Beanie Baby*™ *Bounce*, and its objective is to reinforce location transition words. Shirl has enough Beanie Babies™ for all the students in her class; she collects them and uses them for several classroom activities such as reading buddies or for measuring, sorting, and comparing. Instead, you could use cotton balls, feathers, or even pencils, and just change the name of the activity. Shirl passes out the Beanie Babies™ and then gives directions for the students to follow, using location transition words. She gives directions such as, "Move your Beany Baby™ under your desk," "Move your Beany Baby™ behind your head," "Now put it over your ankle," and "Move your Beany Baby™ above your head and then to the left of your chair." She's found that this activity is especially helpful to her English language learners who need to strengthen their vocabulary and their ability to follow oral directions.

Emotion

Introductory Lessons

To help students use emotion in their writing, Shirl begins, "Writers often try to make their readers have emotion when they read. *Emotion* means feelings. Writers want their readers to feel happy, sad, scared, or mad." She reads the emotions rhyming couplet (see Figure 7.13), and the class chants it several times. She continues, "Today we're going to talk about things that make us happy. When we're happy, we feel good and we often laugh. Let's think about things that make us laugh or smile." Shirl reads several humorous poems (Shel Silverstein's or Jack Prelutsky's are class favorites) or revisits favorite stories to discuss the happy emotions that they evoke. She then pairs students for knee-to-knee discussions to brainstorm things that have made each student happy. See Figure 7.14 for a writing sample from a student's first attempt at using emotions in his writing.

The next three days of the emotions mini-lessons follow the same sequence as the lesson on happy emotions. Shirl first teaches about sad emotions, then scary emotions, and finally emotions of anger. For each

---

EMOTION

Happy, sad, scared, mad—how will your readers feel?
When you write with emotion, your writing
will seem real.

Figure 7.13   Rhyming Couplet for Emotions

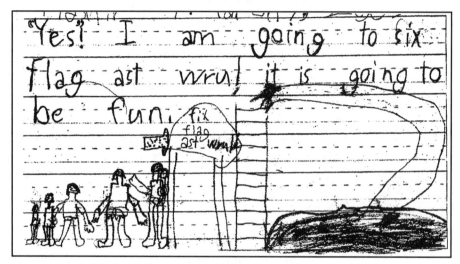

Figure 7.14   Writing With Emotions: *"Yes! I am going to Six Flags Astroworld. It is going to be fun."*

mini-lesson, the class first reviews the emotions rhyming couplet, reads or reviews stories and poems with emotions, and then gets knee-to-knee to discuss emotional moments.

For the last day's lesson on emotions, Shirl gives a target practice assignment. She gives each student a half-sheet of writing paper and tells them to write a short story that makes the reader feel an emotion. She sets a timer for 10 minutes and then collects the papers. After calling the class to the large-group area, she reads several of their pieces aloud. As each piece is read, she asks the students to determine which emotion they felt. The class discusses whether each piece evoked a happy, sad, scary, or angry emotion. The lesson ends as the class chants the emotions rhyming couplet.

Enrichment Activities

During the week(s) that these lessons are taught, Shirl connects these writing workshop skills to books read aloud. After each read aloud opportunity, the students discuss how the story made them feel. To increase their awareness of each writer's craft, Shirl helps the students to identify the words and techniques that each writer uses to bring forth a particular emotion in their readers. This activity continues throughout the year. Figures 7.15 and 7.16 suggest some appropriate titles.

LITERATURE TITLES—EMOTIONS				
Emotion	Title	Author	Publisher	Copy-right Date
Happy	Moira's Birthday	R. Munsch	Annick Press	1987
	The Magic Hat	M. Fox	Harcourt	2002
	Silly Sally	A. Wood	Scholastic	1992
	Tacky the Penguin	H. Lester	Scholastic	1992
Sad	Tough Boris	M. Fox	Harcourt Brace	1992
	The Tenth Good Thing About Barney	J. Viorst	Trumpet Club	1971
	Fly Away Home	E. Bunting	Clarion Books	1991
Scared	There's a Nightmare in My Closet	M. Mayer	Dial Books	1968
	Ira Sleeps Over	B. Waber	Scholastic	1972
	Smoky Night	E. Bunting	Harcourt Brace	1994
Mad	Piggybook	A. Browne	Alfred A. Knopf	1986
	Alexander Who's Not (Do you hear me? I mean it!) Going to Move	J. Viorst	Antheneum Books for Young Readers	1995
	Chicken Sunday	P. Polacco	Scholastic	1992

Figure 7.15   Literature Titles for Teaching Emotions

	POETRY TITLES—EMOTIONS		
	Source: *The Random House Book of Poetry for Children* (Prelutsky, 1983)		
Emotion	**Title**	**Author**	**Page Number**
Happy	"The Reason I Like Chocolate"	Nikki Giovanni	119
	"Ode to Spring"	Walter R. Brooks	42
	"Spring"	Karla Kuskin	43
Sad	"Foghorns"	Lilian Moore	98
	"Since Hanna Moved Away"	Judith Viorst	114
	"Valentine"	Shel Silverstein	38
	"Samuel"	Bobbi Katz	81
	"House. For Sale"	Leonard Clark	162
Scared	"What's That?"	Florence Parry Heide	201
	"When I Was Lost"	Dorothy Aldis	120
	"The Troll"	Jack Prelutsky	206
	"The Bogeyman"	Jack Prelutsky	206
Mad	"Sulk"	Felice Holman	121
	"Leave Me Alone"	Felice Holman	136
Funny	"A Bug Sat in a Silver Flower"	Karla Kuskin	73
	"In the Motel"	X. J. Kennedy	137
	"Way Down South"	Anonymous	173
Sorry	"This is Just to Say"	William Carlos Williams	146
Lonely	"When I Was Lost"	Dorothy Aldis	120
	"The Sugar Lady"	Frank Asch	166
Frustration	"The Wrong Start"	Marchette Chute	132
Brave	"Adventures of Isabel"	Ogden Nash	179
Sibling Rivalry	"My Brother"	Marci Ridlon	136
	"Lil' Bro'"	Karama Fufuka	136

Figure 7.16   Poetry Titles for Teaching Emotions

Emotions Spin is an activity that Shirl uses to reinforce the idea of emotional events. Shirl first has a student spin the emotions spinner. Then a student selects a character from the character bag and describes an event that could occur to the character that would make the character experience the particular emotion selected by the spinner. For example, if the spinner landed on *scared* and the character card selected was *astronaut,* students might brainstorm events such as

- The astronaut heard a rattle in her spacesuit.
- An alien appeared in the window of the spacecraft.
- The astronaut opened the space hatch and stepped into the black open space.

The activity continues as students select both a character and an emotion.

Preparation for Teaching

Resources for Lessons

- Posters:
  - –the large letter *E*
  - –the skills list
  - –the sample sentence
  - –the rhyming couplets for narrow the topic, expand one idea, transition words, and emotion

- Traditional rhymes copied onto transparencies or chart paper:
  - *–Jack and Jill*
  - *–Hickory Dickory Dock*
  - *–Old Mother Hubbard*
  - *–Wee Willie Winkie*
  - *–Little Miss Muffet*
  - *–Humpty Dumpty*

- Suggested book: *The Paperboy* (Pilkey)
- Several poems from the ones suggested in Figure 7.16 copied onto chart paper or transparency

Resources for Enrichment Activities

- Any book or poem from Figures 7.5, 7.6, 7.11, 7.12, 7.15, and 7.16
- Beanie Babies™, cotton balls, pencils, or feathers
- Character cards for *Action Expansion* and *Emotions Spin*
- Emotions spinner for *Emotions Spin*

Chapter

8

Specificity

Figure 8.1 Aashir's Writing

Shirl is pleased with the progress that her students are making in writing. In addition to the craft elements they've already studied, she wants to help them develop skills related to specificity. By using these elements, students learn to be more exact in their descriptions. In Figure 8.1, Aashir has included both a number word and a material word to be more specific.

When we introduce the VOICES category of specificity, we include the skills of using descriptive words (number, color, size, and material words) and proper nouns. We use the sentence "Rover found two big bones under the wooden table." as a sample for all the skills within this category. We also, as always, use an accompanying illustration.

Descriptive Words

Introductory Lessons

To begin instruction is this category, Shirl first introduces the visual aids that accompany this VOICES category. She then says, "When you write a piece, you need to give specific information so that the readers get a crystal-clear picture in their minds. When you're specific, you give exact details. Let's try a little game so you can see what I mean. In your mind, picture a dog. What did you see?" The students discuss the many types of dogs they visualized. Shirl continues, "We all saw different kinds of dogs because just saying 'a dog' isn't very specific. Now picture in your mind a black-and-white dog. That's a little more specific. We know the dog is black and white, but we still don't know specifically what kind of dog it is. Is it little? Is it big? Does it have a black body and a white face, a white body with black spots, or black and white stripes? How long is its tail? We just don't know. Now I will be more specific. Picture in your mind an enormous Dalmatian. Now we know that the dog is black and white. We know that it's big; and because it's a Dalmatian, we know that it is white with small black spots. When we just pictured a dog in our minds, we didn't have enough details to get an exact picture; but when we pictured a Dalmatian, our brains knew exactly what was described. That's what it means to be specific. We give exact details so our readers can know exactly what our writing is describing. Tomorrow we'll start talking about ways to be more specific in our writing." Shirl tells her students to return to their current five-page books.

The second mini-lesson begins as Shirl introduces the rhyming couplet for descriptive words, and she has the students chant it (see Figure 8.2). She then reads the Mother Goose rhyme *Baa, Baa, Black Sheep* written on chart paper. She says, "This nursery rhyme will help us think about being specific. It has some number, size, color, and material words in it. Let's see if we can find a number and color word, and we'll use this tape to highlight them." They then use highlighter tape (you could also use a highlighter marker) to highlight first the number words within the rhyme (*three* bags full) then the color word (*black* sheep). Shirl reminds her students that they have number and color charts already displayed in their classroom. The students complete the target practice by writing and illustrating a sentence that uses both a number and a color word.

```
DESCRIPTIVE WORDS

Add number, size, and color words to be
more specific. Also add material words.
Your writing will be terrific.
```

Figure 8.2 Rhyming Couplet for Descriptive Words

The next lesson begins with a review of the rhyming couplet and the nursery rhyme *Baa, Baa, Black Sheep.* They highlight the size word (*little* boy who lives down the lane). The class then brainstorms words that are used to describe size, and Shirl records these words on a chart. Finally, students write and illustrate a sentence that uses a size word for target practice.

The focus of the next lesson is on material words. First, the class reviews the rhyming couplet and highlights the material word (*wool*) in *Baa, Baa, Black Sheep.* Then Shirl walks around the room and touches items made of different materials (e.g., the table is wood, the file cabinet is metal, the book is paper). (You could even have some fabric swatches to show.) Finally, the class begins a chart to list different material words. Shirl helps the students expand their idea of material words by asking them questions like: What are the materials used to make clothes? Houses? Jewelry? They make a chart similar to the one shown in Figure 8.3. As target practice, Shirl asks the students to write and illustrate a sentence that uses a material word. After completing their target practice, students return to their current five-page books.

MATERIAL WORDS		
CLOTHES	**HOUSES**	**JEWELRY**
wool	brick	gold
cotton	steel	emerald
silk	wood	diamond

Figure 8.3 Chart for Material Words

For the final lesson, Shirl reviews the rhyming couplet and the descriptive word charts that they made in previous lessons. As target practice, Shirl asks the students to write and illustrate a sentence that uses several descriptive words. Her example is, "My little sister bought two silk dresses." After students have completed their target practice (see Figure 8.4), they return to their five-page books.

Figure 8.4 Descriptive Words Target Practice

Enrichment Activities

In addition to using literature and poetry to spotlight descriptive language (see Figures 8.5 and 8.6), Shirl and her students play *I Spy* to practice using specific and descriptive language. She begins by describing something in the classroom and having the children identify what she's described. She makes sure she uses specific descriptors in her sentence. Examples include the following:

- I spy something made of cotton that has thirteen red and white stripes and fifty stars.
- I spy something that has four metal legs and a flat wooden surface.

Once students become familiar with this game, they can make up the riddles for the class.

Descriptions can also be reinforced with the game *Twenty Questions.* The leader selects something in the room and writes the name of the item on a slip of paper. The rest of the class has 20 questions to identify

LITERATURE TITLES—DESCRIPTIVE WORDS			
Title	**Author**	**Publisher**	**Copyright Date**
Sheila Rae's Peppermint Stick	K. Henkes	Greenwillow	2001
Pet Show!	E. J. Keats	Aladdin	1972
Swimmy	L. Lionni	Scholastic	1963
The Relatives Came	C. Rylant	Aladdin	1993
Night in the Country	C. Rylant	Aladdin	1991
Millions of Cats	W. Gag	Coward-McCann	1928
Lunch	D. Fleming	Henry Holt	1992
Planting a Rainbow	L. Ehlert	Harcourt Brace	1988
Who is the Beast?	K. Baker	Harcourt Brace	1990
Five Minute's Peace	J. Murphy	Scholastic	1986
Titch	P. Hutchins	Aladdin	1971
Hazel's Amazing Mother	R. Wells	Scholastic	1985

Figure 8.5 Literature Titles for Teaching Descriptive Words

POETRY TITLES—DESCRIPTIVE WORDS Source: *The Random House Book of Poetry for Children* (Prelutsky, 1983)			
Type of Description	**Title**	**Author**	**Page Number**
Number	"Girls Can, Too!"	Lee Bennett Hopkins	111
	"About Feet"	Margaret Hillert	122
	"Smart"	Shel Silverstein	157
	"The Creature in the Classroom"	Jack Prelutsky	212
Size	"Measurement"	A. M. Sullivan	23
	"Mice"	Rose Fyleman	54
	"The Hippopotamus"	Jack Prelutsky	58
	"Frightening"	Claudia Lewis	98
	"The Story of Augustus Who Would Not Have Any Soup"	Heinrich Hoffmann	107

Figure 8.6 Poetry Titles for Teaching Descriptive Words

(Continued on next page)

POETRY TITLES—DESCRIPTIVE WORDS Source: *The Random House Book of Poetry for Children* (Prelutsky, 1983)			
Type of Description	**Title**	**Author**	**Page Number**
Color	"I'm Glad the Sky is Painted Blue"	Anonymous	22
	"What is Red?"	Mary O'Neill	219
	"The Blackbird"	Humbert Wolfe	83
	"The Marrog"	R. C. Scriven	125
	"Growing Older"	Rose Henderson	159
	"Yellow"	David McCord	220
	"Winter Clothes"	Karla Kuskin	128
Material	"The Library"	Barbara A. Huff	220
	"Rules"	Karla Kuskin	137
	"Paper Dragons"	Susan Alton Schmeltz	40
	"Huckleberry, Gooseberry, Raspberry Pie"	Clyde Watson	103
	"McIntosh Apple"	Steven Kroll	171

Figure 8.6   Poetry Titles for Teaching Descriptive Words *(Continued)*

the item. For this enrichment activity, the questions must contain number, size, color, or material words.

Freeman (1998) suggests an activity called the *General-to-Specific Game*, and Shirl's students enjoy it. The directions are as follows:

- Students sit on the floor or in their chairs.
- Shirl says a general word, such as "game."
- Shirl calls on one student to respond with a more specific word, such as "football," "checkers," or "Red Rover."
- After offering a specific replacement for a general word, the child stands up.
- The game ends when all children are standing.

After the game has been played, Shirl and her students make a list similar to the one shown in Figure 8.7.

In addition to the other enrichment activities, Shirl also wants to expand her students' use of descriptive words by helping them identify synonyms for the typical words they use. One activity is called *Word Ladders*. (We thank our colleague Cindy Cecil for this idea.) Shirl writes a

SPECIFICITY	
GENERAL	SPECIFIC
Flowers	• rose, tulip, daisy, magnolia . . .
Games	• football, checkers, chess . . .
Drinks	• milk, water, juice . . .
Fruit	• pear, peach, banana . . .
Snack	• crackers, popcorn, apple . . .

Figure 8.7   General-to-Specific Chart

common word on a card (for example, *good*), and the class writes other words that mean the same or nearly the same on cards of a different color (such as, *grand, amazing, great,* or *fine*). Then they are displayed vertically to form a ladder (see Figure 8.8).

Figure 8.8   Word Ladders

An activity similar to Word Ladders is to collect synonyms in a class-made *Synonym Dictionary*. As seen in Figure 8.9, the key word is written in the box and up to four synonyms are written on the lines. Shirl makes the pages available for her students to use as they identify synonyms (see appendix C). She collects these in a book made with a construction paper cover. So that it's easy to add sheets, she connects the pages with metal rings.

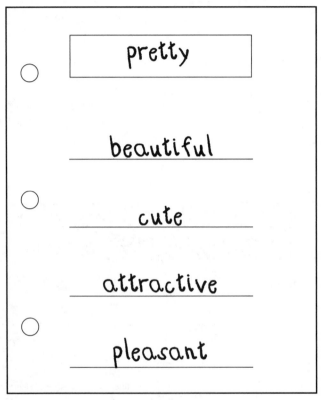

Figure 8.9 Page of Synonym Dictionary

Proper Nouns

Introductory Lessons

Shirl introduces this writing skill by beginning with the rhyming couplet (see Figure 8.10). She says, "Today's rhyme is about using proper nouns to be more specific. A proper noun is the name of a person or a place. Let's say our rhyme together." After the class reads the rhyme several times, Shirl continues, "I could write about my friend, but I'm more specific if I give my friend's name—*Dawn*. I could write about my visit to the doctor, but I'm more specific when I use a proper noun—*Dr. Wolf*. I could write about the city I live in, but instead of saying *city*, I could say *Houston*. Using a proper noun makes my writing more specific." Just as she did during her first lesson on number, color, size, and material words, Shirl helps her students show that using a proper noun enables the brain to get a more exact picture. She uses the following sentence sequence:

> Mom went to the store.
>
> Mom went to the grocery store.
>
> Mom went to Walmart Supercenter.

The class uses these sentences to discuss how the proper noun gives the reader a better picture of where Mom went shopping. After they chant the rhyming couplet again, Shirl reminds her students to look for proper nouns in their reading and writing. Students then continue working in their current five-page books.

PROPER NOUNS

**Be a name dropper.
Use a noun that is proper.**

Figure 8.10   Rhyming Couplet for Proper Nouns

The second mini-lesson on proper nouns begins with a review of the previous day's lesson and a recitation of the rhyming couplet. Shirl then uses a familiar nursery rhyme to show the difference that a proper noun makes. She says, "I know you like the nursery rhyme *Humpty Dumpty*." The class says the nursery rhyme together. Shirl continues, "Let's see how it would sound without a proper noun. 'The egg sat on the wall. The egg had a great fall. All the king's horses and all the king's men couldn't put the egg together again.'" She leads the class in a discussion about how the rhyme is more interesting and specific with the proper noun added. Next, Shirl places an unlit candle in a candlestick on the floor and recites the nursery rhyme *Jack Be Nimble*. Shirl also takes this opportunity to review strong verbs by discussing alternatives for the word *jump*. Then she says, "We can use this nursery rhyme to have some fun with proper nouns. When I say the rhyme with your proper name instead of Jack's, you can stand up and tell us the strong verb you want to act out. Then you can jump over the candlestick showing us your strong verb." (An example is, "Mary be nimble, Mary be quick, Mary slithered around the candlestick.") As a rhyme is chanted, each child acts it out.

After reciting the rhyming couplet, Shirl begins the third mini-lesson by beginning a proper noun chart and brainstorming specific names for each category (see Figure 8.11). (The category options are numerous; choose the ones that will interest your students.) Shirl uses this occasion to reinforce students' use of capital letters for proper nouns. The lesson ends with target practice. Shirl directs the students to write a sentence that uses proper nouns. Her sample sentence is "On Sunday, Mary drove to Walmart." She tells her students they can use the frame sentence, "On ____, ____ drove to ____." if they choose. When students are finished with target practice, they continue working on their five-page books. Two students' use of proper nouns as seen in Figures 8.12 and 8.13.

PROPER NOUNS					
Stores	Restaurants	Cities	Countries	Book Characters	Friends

Figure 8.11   Categories of Proper Nouns

Figure 8.12   Independent Use of Proper Nouns

Figure 8.13   Independent Use of Material Words and Proper Nouns

Enrichment Activities

As always, Shirl uses literature and poetry to review proper nouns (see Figures 8.14 and 8.15). She also plays the *I Spy* game described in the section on descriptive words, but in this instance Shirl's answers include proper names (e.g., I spy someone who has on a blue denim shirt with

LITERATURE TITLES—PROPER NOUNS			
Title	**Author**	**Publisher**	**Copyright Date**
A Chair for My Mother	V. B. Williams	Scholastic	1982
Best Friends	S. Kellogg	Dial Book for Young Readers	1986
Little Louie the Baby Bloomer	R. Krauss	HarperCollins	1998
Cookie's Week	C. Ward	Scholastic	1988
Mice and Beans	P. Ryan	Scholastic	2001

Figure 8.14   Literature Titles for Teaching Proper Nouns

Title	Author	Page Number
"Valentine"	Shel Silverstein	38
"Samuel"	Bobbi Katz	81
"Eat-It-All Elaine"	Kaye Starbird	108
"How to Get There"	Bonnie Nims	121
"The Months"	Sara Coleridge	36
"Wendy in Winter"	Kaye Starbird	109
"Since Hanna Moved Away"	Judith Viorst	114
"Far Trek"	Jane Brady	225

POETRY TITLES—PROPER NOUNS
Source: *The Random House Book of Poetry for Children* (Prelutsky, 1983)

Figure 8.15   Poetry Titles for Teaching Proper Nouns

seven white buttons. I spy someone who is four feet tall and has red hair and green eyes.) In addition, students can play the game with partners.

Newspaper Sort is another activity, though the students need to be fairly accomplished readers to do this activity well. Shirl provides her students with newspapers and asks them to cut out several proper nouns. Sometimes she specifies the categories; and at other times, she leaves the categories open-ended. Once the proper nouns are cut out, students sort the words into categories, glue them on to a piece of paper, and label the categories (see Figure 8.16).

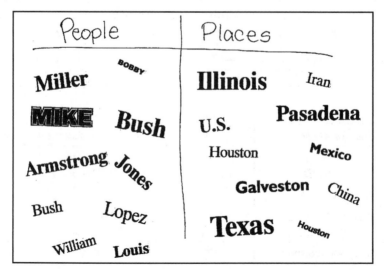

Figure 8.16   Proper Nouns Newspaper Sort

Shirl completes all the VOICES lessons in order, so she typically doesn't teach the mini-lessons on proper nouns until late in the school year. However, she knows that she can prepare students for these writing workshop lessons by introducing them to proper nouns during other language arts lessons earlier in the year. Using a teaching sequence similar to the one presented in Figure 8.17, Shirl focuses on the different proper noun categories during read alouds, shared reading, shared writing, interactive writing, and modeled writing.

TEACHING SEQUENCE FOR PROPER NOUNS	
Month	**Skill**
September	• I • Books (as they are discussed)
October	• Names (friends, family members, pets, teachers, cartoon characters, etc.)
November	• Days of the Week • Months of the Year
December	• Stores • Restaurants
January	• Continents • Countries
February	• Products (brand names for toys, cereal, shoes, snacks, cars, etc.)
March	• Cities • States
April	• Holidays • Planets
May	• Geographic Locations (mountains, lakes, rivers, oceans)

Figure 8.17 Optional Teaching Sequence for Proper Nouns

Once students are familiar with descriptive words and proper nouns, Shirl introduces an activity called *Specificity Spin*. A student selects a character card and spins the descriptive words spinner. Students then brainstorm sentences that describe the character in some way. Examples include the following:

Number:	The six astronauts were in the space shuttle.
Color:	The astronaut gazed at the silver moon.
Material:	The astronaut wore her rubber boots.
Size:	The astronaut's suit was huge.

Proper noun: Danny Richards helped fix the broken space telescope.

Preparation for Teaching

Resources for Lessons

- Posters:
  - the large letter *S*
  - the skills list
  - the sample sentence
  - the rhyming couplets for descriptive words and proper nouns
- Traditional rhymes copied onto transparencies or chart paper:
  - *Baa, Baa, Black Sheep*
  - *Humpty Dumpty*
  - *Jack Be Nimble*

Resources for Enrichment Activities

- Any book or poem from Figures 8.5, 8.6, 8.14, and 8.15
- Index cards for *Word Ladders*
- *Synonym Dictionary* sheets from appendix C
- Newspapers for *Newspaper Sort*
- Character cards and descriptive words spinner for *Specificity Spin*

Chapter 9

Sustaining VOICES

The lessons we've described in this book will require many opportunities for reinforcement and encouragement so that students begin to use the skills in their own writing. During any of the VOICES lessons, a few students will only be at the recognition stage of development; that is, they can recognize the skill in the books they read but they aren't yet ready to use them routinely in their writing. Most students will recognize the VOICES skills and use them often, sometimes with reminders from you. You'll even have a few students who gobble up the ideas presented in this chapter and overuse them. That's okay—as they grow as writers, they'll develop more maturity in their writing and use the skills more judiciously.

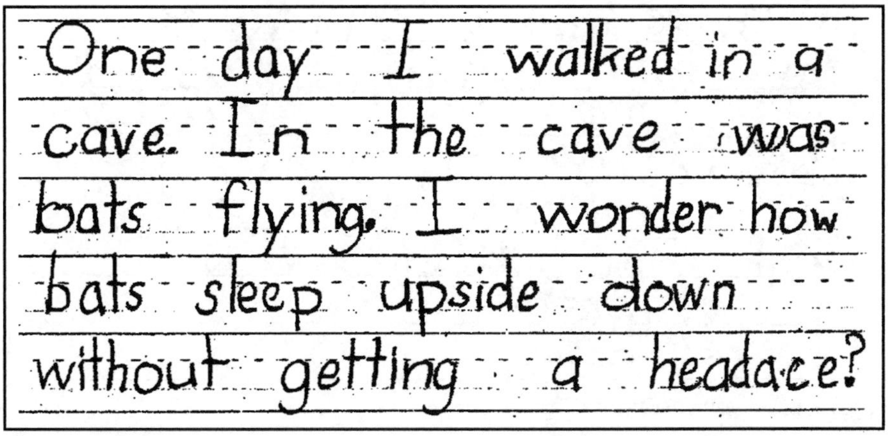

One day I walked in a cave. In the cave was bats flying. I wonder how bats sleep upside down without getting a headace?

Figure 9.1 Irene's Writing

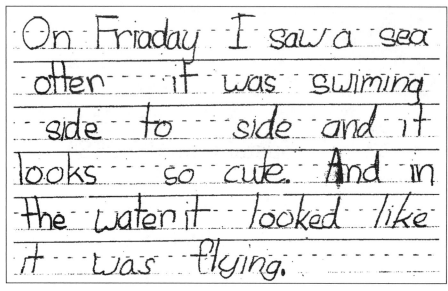

On Friaday I saw a sea otter it was swiming side to side and it looks so cute. And in the water it looked like it was flying.

Figure 9.2 Bianca's Writing

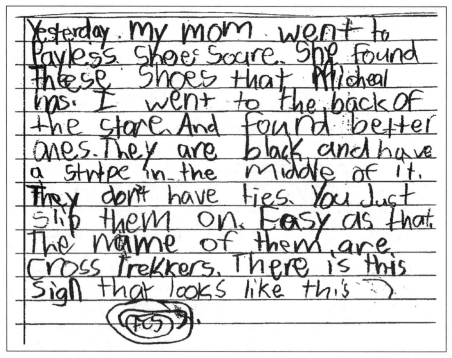

Yesterday my mom went to Payless Shoe Soare. She found these shoes that Micheal has. I went to the back of the store. And found better ones. They are black and have a stripe in the middle of it. They don't have ties. You just slip them on. Easy as that. The name of them are Cross Trekkers. There is this sign that looks like this

Figure 9.3 John's Writing

The three student samples that accompany this chapter help us illustrate the kinds of writing that primary students can do with systematic instruction, structure, support, and encouragement. As shown in these examples, the students used vivid word choice, comparisons, emotions, descriptive and specific words, and other effective craft elements. The samples were taken from students in Shirl's first-grade class.

Our VOICES structure provides a framework in which to introduce and discuss concepts related to the author's craft, and it helps teachers to guide their young writers as the students develop their writing skills. However, these lessons alone do not make a total writing program. Primary writers need modeling, small group instruction, response opportunities, systematic assessment, and lessons on procedures and conventions. In addition, the VOICES lessons alone will not be enough to keep the ideas foremost in students' minds as they write. Instead, to sustain the VOICES skills, teachers must keep them alive. We can do this by locating them in familiar books, modeling their use through our own writing, revisiting them in mini-lessons, and using the VOICES board for routine review and discussion. We can celebrate with our students when we see the VOICES skills used in their writing. As primary teachers, we don't expect to see our students become sophisticated authors who write with complex plots. However, we will hear their own voices shine through in their writings as we work to maintain their understanding of VOICES.

Appendices

Appendix A—VOICES Board

- Large Letter
- Categories
- Sample Sentence
- Icon
- Rhyming Couplets

Appendix B—Traditional Rhymes

Appendix C—Resources for Enrichment Activities

Appendix

A

VOICES Board

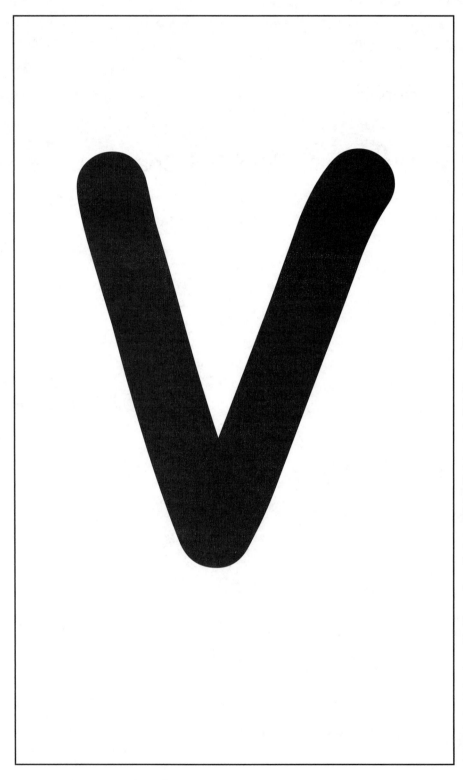

© 2003 by D. Rickards and S. Hawes from *Exploring Writing Workshop in the K–2 Classroom: Discovering Our VOICES*. Norwood, MA: Christopher-Gordon.

© 2003 by D. Rickards and S. Hawes from *Exploring Writing Workshop in the K–2 Classroom: Discovering Our VOICES.* Norwood, MA: Christopher-Gordon.

VIVID WORD CHOICE

*Strong verbs
*Leads
*Endings

The frog leaped over the log.

© 2003 by D. Rickards and S. Hawes from *Exploring Writing Workshop in the K–2 Classroom: Discovering Our VOICES.* Norwood, MA: Christopher-Gordon.

© 2003 by D. Rickards and S. Hawes from *Exploring Writing Workshop in the K–2 Classroom: Discovering Our VOICES.* Norwood, MA: Christopher-Gordon.

STRONG VERBS

A strong verb shows how to move or speak.

Use action words to be strong, not weak.

© 2003 by D. Rickards and S. Hawes from *Exploring Writing Workshop in the K–2 Classroom: Discovering Our VOICES*. Norwood, MA: Christopher-Gordon.

© 2003 by D. Rickards and S. Hawes from *Exploring Writing Workshop in the K–2 Classroom: Discovering Our VOICES*. Norwood, MA: Christopher-Gordon.

LEADS

A good lead is like a hook.

It makes your reader take a look.

ENDINGS

Use a big surprise, a circle, or a feeling

To write a good ending that's much more appealing.

© 2003 by D. Rickards and S. Hawes from *Exploring Writing Workshop in the K–2 Classroom: Discovering Our VOICES*. Norwood, MA: Christopher-Gordon.

© 2003 by D. Rickards and S. Hawes from *Exploring Writing Workshop in the K–2 Classroom: Discovering Our VOICES*. Norwood, MA: Christopher-Gordon.

ONOMATOPOEIA

*Onomatopoeia
*Alliteration

© 2003 by D. Rickards and S. Hawes from *Exploring Writing Workshop in the K–2 Classroom: Discovering Our VOICES.* Norwood, MA: Christopher-Gordon.

Splash! The duck dives deep into the pond.

© 2003 by D. Rickards and S. Hawes from *Exploring Writing Workshop in the K–2 Classroom: Discovering Our VOICES*. Norwood, MA: Christopher-Gordon.

© 2003 by D. Rickards and S. Hawes from *Exploring Writing Workshop in the K–2 Classroom: Discovering Our VOICES*. Norwood, MA: Christopher-Gordon.

© 2003 by D. Rickards and S. Hawes from *Exploring Writing Workshop in the K–2 Classroom: Discovering Our VOICES.* Norwood, MA: Christopher-Gordon.

ONOMATOPOEIA

"Crash – bang – thump –
screech – sizzle – tweet!"

Onomatopoeia is
a noisy treat.

ALLITERATION

Alliteration sounds so sweet.

It's a sound that does repeat.

© 2003 by D. Rickards and S. Hawes from *Exploring Writing Workshop in the K–2 Classroom: Discovering Our VOICES.* Norwood, MA: Christopher-Gordon.

© 2003 by D. Rickards and S. Hawes from *Exploring Writing Workshop in the K–2 Classroom: Discovering Our VOICES.* Norwood, MA: Christopher-Gordon.

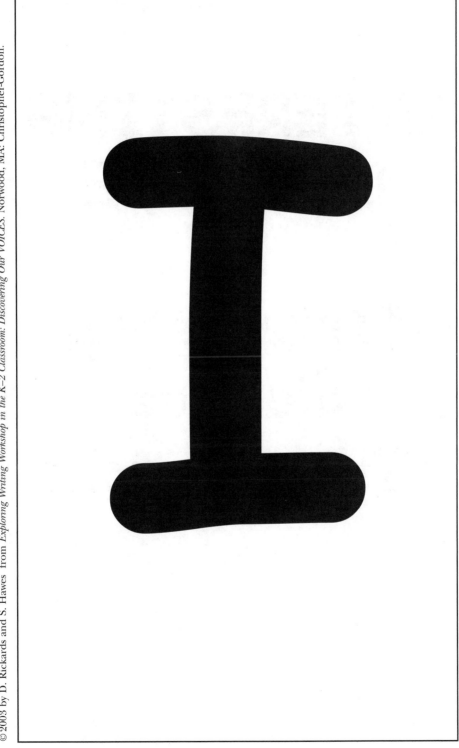

INTERESTING DIALOGUE

*Interesting dialogue
*Interjections

© 2003 by D. Rickards and S. Hawes from *Exploring Writing Workshop in the K–2 Classroom: Discovering Our VOICES.* Norwood, MA: Christopher-Gordon.

"Wow! Look at that bug," said Tom.

Billy said, "It's a huge cricket."

© 2003 by D. Rickards and S. Hawes from *Exploring Writing Workshop in the K–2 Classroom: Discovering Our VOICES*. Norwood, MA: Christopher-Gordon.

© 2003 by D. Rickards and S. Hawes from *Exploring Writing Workshop in the K–2 Classroom: Discovering Our VOICES.* Norwood, MA: Christopher-Gordon.

© 2003 by D. Rickards and S. Hawes from *Exploring Writing Workshop in the K–2 Classroom: Discovering Our VOICES.* Norwood, MA: Christopher-Gordon.

INTERESTING DIALOGUE

You use dialogue
to show conversation.

Then you add
special punctuation.

INTERJECTIONS

"Wow!" cried the writer when he used an interjection.

"Making writing more exciting is a good suggestion."

© 2003 by D. Rickards and S. Hawes from *Exploring Writing Workshop in the K–2 Classroom: Discovering Our VOICES*. Norwood, MA: Christopher-Gordon.

© 2003 by D. Rickards and S. Hawes from *Exploring Writing Workshop in the K–2 Classroom: Discovering Our VOICES*. Norwood, MA: Christopher-Gordon.

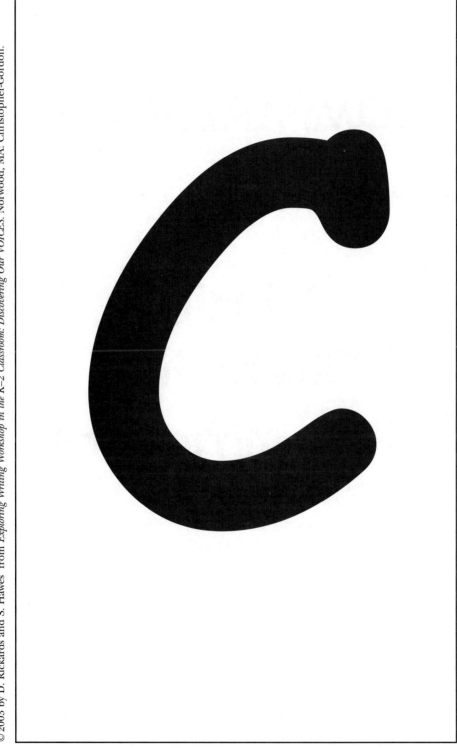

COMPARISONS

*Simile
*Metaphor
*Personification

© 2003 by D. Rickards and S. Hawes from *Exploring Writing Workshop in the K–2 Classroom: Discovering Our VOICES.* Norwood, MA: Christopher-Gordon.

© 2003 by D. Rickards and S. Hawes from *Exploring Writing Workshop in the K–2 Classroom: Discovering Our VOICES*. Norwood, MA: Christopher-Gordon.

The rain played a sad song on my head. My hair felt like a wet mop.

© 2003 by D. Rickards and S. Hawes from *Exploring Writing Workshop in the K–2 Classroom: Discovering Our VOICES.* Norwood, MA: Christopher-Gordon.

© 2003 by D. Rickards and S. Hawes from *Exploring Writing Workshop in the K–2 Classroom: Discovering Our VOICES*. Norwood, MA: Christopher-Gordon.

SIMILE

When you use "like" or "as" to compare,

A simile makes writing as strong as a bear.

METAPHOR

A metaphor is a window into your book.

When you compare two things, you get a better look.

© 2003 by D. Rickards and S. Hawes from *Exploring Writing Workshop in the K–2 Classroom: Discovering Our VOICES*. Norwood, MA: Christopher-Gordon.

© 2003 by D. Rickards and S. Hawes from *Exploring Writing Workshop in the K–2 Classroom: Discovering Our VOICES*. Norwood, MA: Christopher-Gordon.

PERSONIFICATION

"The sun smiles down on me," is personification.

To make animals and things act like people, use your imagination.

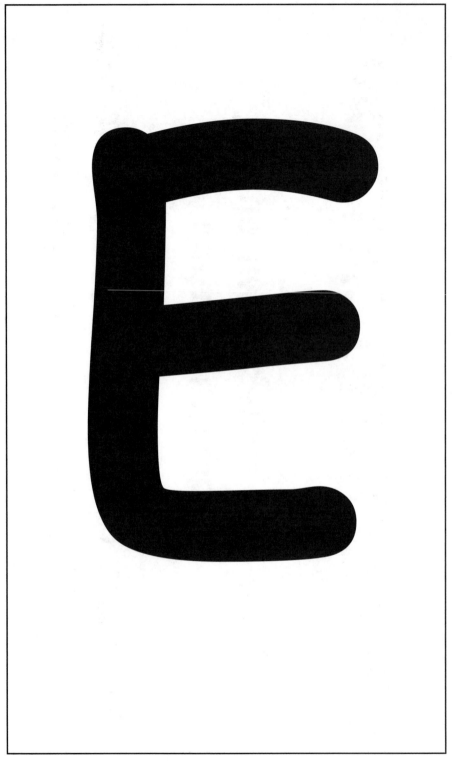

© 2003 by D. Rickards and S. Hawes from *Exploring Writing Workshop in the K–2 Classroom: Discovering Our VOICES*. Norwood, MA: Christopher-Gordon.

© 2003 by D. Rickards and S. Hawes from *Exploring Writing Workshop in the K–2 Classroom: Discovering Our VOICES*. Norwood, MA: Christopher-Gordon.

EXPAND ONE IDEA

*Expand one idea
*Narrow the topic
*Transition words
*Emotions

Suddenly, a door creaked open. Out slithered an enormous dragon.

© 2003 by D. Rickards and S. Hawes from *Exploring Writing Workshop in the K–2 Classroom: Discovering Our VOICES*. Norwood, MA: Christopher-Gordon.

© 2003 by D. Rickards and S. Hawes from *Exploring Writing Workshop in the K–2 Classroom: Discovering Our VOICES.* Norwood, MA: Christopher-Gordon.

NARROW THE TOPIC

Narrow your topic.
Write about one thing.

You don't have to write about everything.

© 2003 by D. Rickards and S. Hawes from *Exploring Writing Workshop in the K–2 Classroom: Discovering Our VOICES*. Norwood, MA: Christopher-Gordon.

© 2003 by D. Rickards and S. Hawes from *Exploring Writing Workshop in the K–2 Classroom: Discovering Our VOICES.* Norwood, MA: Christopher-Gordon.

EXPAND ONE IDEA

When you expand one idea with useful information –

like "who, what, when, where, how, and why" – you'll improve communication.

TRANSITION WORDS

"And then," "and then,"
"and then," "and then"
gets a little boring.

Use other transition words so your
readers won't be snoring.

© 2003 by D. Rickards and S. Hawes from *Exploring Writing Workshop in the K–2 Classroom: Discovering Our VOICES*. Norwood, MA: Christopher-Gordon.

© 2003 by D. Rickards and S. Hawes from *Exploring Writing Workshop in the K–2 Classroom: Discovering Our VOICES.* Norwood, MA: Christopher-Gordon.

EMOTION

Happy, sad, scared, mad – how will your readers feel?

When you write with emotion, your writing will seem real.

© 2003 by D. Rickards and S. Hawes from *Exploring Writing Workshop in the K–2 Classroom: Discovering Our VOICES*. Norwood, MA: Christopher-Gordon.

© 2003 by D. Rickards and S. Hawes from *Exploring Writing Workshop in the K–2 Classroom: Discovering Our VOICES*. Norwood, MA: Christopher-Gordon.

SPECIFICITY

*Descriptive words
*Proper nouns

Rover found two big bones under the wooden table.

© 2003 by D. Rickards and S. Hawes from *Exploring Writing Workshop in the K–2 Classroom: Discovering Our VOICES.* Norwood, MA: Christopher-Gordon.

© 2003 by D. Rickards and S. Hawes from *Exploring Writing Workshop in the K–2 Classroom: Discovering Our VOICES.* Norwood, MA: Christopher-Gordon.

DESCRIPTIVE WORDS

Add number, size, and color words to be more specific.

Also add material words. Your writing will be terrific.

© 2003 by D. Rickards and S. Hawes from *Exploring Writing Workshop in the K–2 Classroom: Discovering Our VOICES*. Norwood, MA: Christopher-Gordon.

PROPER NOUNS

Be a name dropper.

Use a noun that is proper.

© 2003 by D. Rickards and S. Hawes from *Exploring Writing Workshop in the K–2 Classroom: Discovering Our VOICES.* Norwood, MA: Christopher-Gordon.

Appendix

B   Traditional Rhymes

Baa, Baa, Black Sheep

Baa, baa, black sheep,
Have you any wool?
Yes, sir. Yes, sir.
Three bags full.

© 2003 by D. Rickards and S. Hawes from *Exploring Writing Workshop in the K–2 Classroom: Discovering Our VOICES*. Norwood, MA: Christopher-Gordon.

© 2003 by D. Rickards and S. Hawes from *Exploring Writing Workshop in the K–2 Classroom: Discovering Our VOICES*. Norwood, MA: Christopher-Gordon.

The Bear Went Over the Mountain

The bear went over the mountain,
The bear went over the mountain,
The bear went over the mountain
To see what he could see.

Betty Botter's Butter

Betty Botter bought some butter,
but the butter tasted bitter.
So she bought a bit of butter
better than her bitter butter.
She put the butter in her batter,
and the batter was not bitter.
So . . . . it was better Betty Botter
bought a bit of better butter.

© 2003 by D. Rickards and S. Hawes from *Exploring Writing Workshop in the K–2 Classroom: Discovering Our VOICES.* Norwood, MA: Christopher-Gordon.

© 2003 by D. Rickards and S. Hawes from *Exploring Writing Workshop in the K–2 Classroom: Discovering Our VOICES.* Norwood, MA: Christopher-Gordon.

Five Little Monkeys

Five little monkeys jumping
on the bed.

One fell off and bumped his head.

Mama called the doctor,

and the doctor said,

"No more monkeys jumping
on the bed."

Hey Diddle Diddle

Hey diddle diddle,
The cat and the fiddle,
The cow jumped over the moon.
The little dog laughed
to see such sport.
And the dish ran away
with the spoon.

© 2003 by D. Rickards and S. Hawes from *Exploring Writing Workshop in the K–2 Classroom: Discovering Our VOICES.* Norwood, MA: Christopher-Gordon.

© 2003 by D. Rickards and S. Hawes from *Exploring Writing Workshop in the K–2 Classroom: Discovering Our VOICES.* Norwood, MA: Christopher-Gordon.

Hickory, Dickory, Dock

Hickory, dickory, dock.
The mouse ran up the clock.
The clock struck one,
And down he ran.
Hickory, dickory dock.

Humpty Dumpty

Humpty Dumpty sat on a wall.
Humpty Dumpty had a great fall.
All the king's horses
And all the king's men
Couldn't put Humpty
together again.

© 2003 by D. Rickards and S. Hawes from *Exploring Writing Workshop in the K–2 Classroom: Discovering Our VOICES.* Norwood, MA: Christopher-Gordon.

© 2003 by D. Rickards and S. Hawes from *Exploring Writing Workshop in the K–2 Classroom: Discovering Our VOICES.* Norwood, MA: Christopher-Gordon.

I'm a Little Teapot

I'm a little teapot, short and stout.

Here is my handle. Here is my spout.

When I get all steamed up,

I will shout,

"Just tip me over and pour me out."

Jack and Jill

Jack and Jill went up the hill
To fetch a pail of water.

Jack fell down and broke his crown
And Jill came tumbling after.

© 2003 by D. Rickards and S. Hawes from *Exploring Writing Workshop in the K–2 Classroom: Discovering Our VOICES*. Norwood, MA: Christopher-Gordon.

© 2003 by D. Rickards and S. Hawes from *Exploring Writing Workshop in the K–2 Classroom: Discovering Our VOICES.* Norwood, MA: Christopher-Gordon.

Jack Be Nimble

Jack be nimble.

Jack be quick.

Jack jumped over the candlestick.

Little Bo Peep

Little Bo Peep has lost her sheep
And can't tell where to find them.
Leave them alone
And they'll come home,
Wagging their tails behind them.

© 2003 by D. Rickards and S. Hawes from *Exploring Writing Workshop in the K–2 Classroom: Discovering Our VOICES.* Norwood, MA: Christopher-Gordon.

© 2003 by D. Rickards and S. Hawes from *Exploring Writing Workshop in the K–2 Classroom: Discovering Our VOICES*. Norwood, MA: Christopher-Gordon.

Little Miss Muffet

Little Miss Muffet sat on a tuffet
Eating her curds and whey.

Along came a spider
And sat down beside her,
And frightened Miss Muffet away.

Little Miss Muffet (revised)

Little Miss Muffet sat on a tuffet
Eating her curds and whey.

Along came a spider
And sat down beside her.
And then Miss Muffet went home.

© 2003 by D. Rickards and S. Hawes from *Exploring Writing Workshop in the K–2 Classroom: Discovering Our VOICES.* Norwood, MA: Christopher-Gordon.

© 2003 by D. Rickards and S. Hawes from *Exploring Writing Workshop in the K–2 Classroom: Discovering Our VOICES.* Norwood, MA: Christopher-Gordon.

Mary Had a Little Lamb

Mary had a little lamb.

Its fleece was white as snow.

And everywhere that Mary went,

The lamb was sure to go.

Mary, Mary, Quite Contrary

Mary, Mary, quite contrary,
How does your garden grow?
With silver bells and cockle shells
And pretty maidens all in a row.

© 2003 by D. Rickards and S. Hawes from *Exploring Writing Workshop in the K–2 Classroom: Discovering Our VOICES*. Norwood, MA: Christopher-Gordon.

© 2003 by D. Rickards and S. Hawes from *Exploring Writing Workshop in the K–2 Classroom: Discovering Our VOICES.* Norwood, MA: Christopher-Gordon.

Old Mother Hubbard

Old Mother Hubbard
Went to the cupboard
To get her poor dog a bone.
But when she got there,
The cupboard was bare.
And so her poor dog had none.

Peter Piper

Peter Piper picked a peck
of pickled peppers.
If Peter Piper picked a peck
of pickled peppers,
how many pickled peppers
did Peter Piper pick?

© 2003 by D. Rickards and S. Hawes from *Exploring Writing Workshop in the K–2 Classroom: Discovering Our VOICES.* Norwood, MA: Christopher-Gordon.

© 2003 by D. Rickards and S. Hawes from *Exploring Writing Workshop in the K–2 Classroom: Discovering Our VOICES*. Norwood, MA: Christopher-Gordon.

There Was an Old Woman

There was an old woman
Who lived in a shoe.
She had so many children,
She didn't know what to do.

Three Little Kittens

Three little kittens have lost their mittens,

And they begin to cry.

"Oh! Mother dear, we sadly fear,

our mittens we we have lost."

© 2003 by D. Rickards and S. Hawes from *Exploring Writing Workshop in the K–2 Classroom: Discovering Our VOICES*. Norwood, MA: Christopher-Gordon.

© 2003 by D. Rickards and S. Hawes from *Exploring Writing Workshop in the K–2 Classroom: Discovering Our VOICES.* Norwood, MA: Christopher-Gordon.

Twinkle, Twinkle, Little Star

Twinkle, twinkle, little star.
How I wonder what you are.
Up above the world so high,
Like a diamond in the sky.
Twinkle, twinkle, little star.
How I wonder what you are.

Wee Willie Winkie

Wee Willie Winkie
Went through town,
Upstairs and downstairs
In his nightgown.

© 2003 by D. Rickards and S. Hawes from *Exploring Writing Workshop in the K–2 Classroom: Discovering Our VOICES*. Norwood, MA: Christopher-Gordon.

Appendix

C

Resources for Enrichment Activities

ONOMATOPOEIA MATCH-UP

Animals

Onomatopoeia	Source
Who-o-o-o-o-o	Owl
Me-ow	Cat
Arf-arf	Dog
Cluck	Chicken
Quack	Duck
Neigh	Horse
Moo	Cow
Oink	Pig

Other

Onomatopoeia	Source
Ding Dong	Doorbell
Vroom	Race car
Toot toot	Horn
Splash	Water
Tick-tock	Clock
Clip-clop	Horse's hooves
Rip	Paper
Zip	Zipper

© 2003 by D. Rickards and S. Hawes from *Exploring Writing Workshop in the K–2 Classroom: Discovering Our VOICES*. Norwood, MA: Christopher-Gordon.

Alliteration Readers Theater

Peter Piper

Reader 1:   Presenting 'Peter Piper'—a tongue twister.

Reader 2:   Peter Piper picked a peck of pickled peppers.

Reader 1:   If Peter Piper picked a peck of pickled peppers,

Reader 2:   How many pickled peppers did Peter Piper pick?

© 2003 by D. Rickards and S. Hawes from *Exploring Writing Workshop in the K–2 Classroom: Discovering Our VOICES*. Norwood, MA: Christopher-Gordon.

Alliteration Readers Theater

Betty Botter's Butter

Reader 1:   Presenting a tongue twister – 'Betty Botter's Butter.'

Reader 2:   Betty Botter bought some butter.

Reader 1:   But the butter tasted bitter.

Reader 2:   So she bought a bit of butter better than her bitter butter.

Reader 1:   She put the butter in her batter, and the batter was not bitter.

All: So . . .

Reader 2:   It was better Betty Botter bought a bit of better butter.

© 2003 by D. Rickards and S. Hawes from *Exploring Writing Workshop in the K–2 Classroom: Discovering Our VOICES*. Norwood, MA: Christopher-Gordon.

Little Miss Muffet
(a Readers Theater script)

© 2003 by D. Rickards and S. Hawes from *Exploring Writing Workshop in the K–2 Classroom: Discovering Our VOICES.* Norwood, MA: Christopher-Gordon.

Narrator: Little Miss Muffet sat on a tuffet.

Muffet: I think I'll sit down and eat some curds and whey.

Narrator: She began to eat.

Muffet: Yum, yum. I like curds and whey.

Narrator: Along came a spider.

Spider: I'll sit down beside her.

Muffet: Eek! I hate spiders!

Spider: I frightened Miss Muffet away.

Humpty Dumpty
(a Readers Theater script)

Narrator: Humpty Dumpty sat on a wall.

Humpty: I think I'll climb up here and see what I can see.

Narrator: Humpty Dumpty had a great fall.

Humpty: Oh, no! I'm losing my balance! Ouch!

Narrator: All the king's horses and all the king's men came to help.

King's Man: We can't put Humpty together again.

© 2003 by D. Rickards and S. Hawes from *Exploring Writing Workshop in the K–2 Classroom: Discovering Our VOICES.* Norwood, MA: Christopher-Gordon.

© 2003 by D. Rickards and S. Hawes from *Exploring Writing Workshop in the K–2 Classroom: Discovering Our VOICES*. Norwood, MA: Christopher-Gordon.

The Three Little Pigs
(a Readers Theater script)

Narrator:　　Once upon a time, there were three little pigs.

Pig 1:　　I will build my house out of straw.

Pig 2:　　I think I'll use sticks.

Pig 3.　　I want to use bricks to make my house safe and strong.

Narrator:　　So the three little pigs got busy building their houses. Then the big bad wolf came by the house of the first little pig.

Wolf:　　Little pig, little pig, let me come in.

Pig 1:　　Not by the hair of my chinny-chin-chin.

Wolf:　　Then I'll huff, and I'll puff, and I'll blow your house down.

Narrator:　　And that is what he did. The first little pig ran to his brother's stick house. The big bad wolf went there, too.

Wolf:　　Little pigs, little pigs, let me come in.

Pig 1 and Pig 2:	Not by the hair of our chinny-chin-chins.
Wolf:	Then I'll huff, and I'll puff, and I'll blow your house down.
Narrator:	And that is what he did again. The little pigs ran to their brother's brick house. The big bad wolf went there, too.
Wolf:	Little pigs, little pigs, let me come in.
All three pigs:	Not by the hair of our chinny-chin-chins.
Wolf:	Then I'll huff, and I'll puff, and I'll blow your house down.
Narrator:	He huffed and puffed, but he couldn't blow the strong brick house down. He decided to go down the chimney.
Pig 3:	Quick, brothers. Let's build a fire in the fireplace.
Narrator:	The fire frightened the wolf and he ran away.
Wolf:	I'll never bother those three little pigs again.

© 2003 by D. Rickards and S. Hawes from *Exploring Writing Workshop in the K–2 Classroom: Discovering Our VOICES.* Norwood, MA: Christopher-Gordon.

Interjection Match-Up

Interjection	Matching Sentence
Whee!	This roller coaster is fun!
Ouch!	I hurt my knee.
Whoa!	Slow down!
Oops!	I dropped my glass.
Yahoo!	My team won the game.
Yum!	That cake tastes great.
Yuck!	The garbage smells bad.
Whew!	It's hot.

© 2003 by D. Rickards and S. Hawes from *Exploring Writing Workshop in the K–2 Classroom: Discovering Our VOICES.* Norwood, MA: Christopher-Gordon.

Synonyms

© 2003 by D. Rickards and S. Hawes from *Exploring Writing Workshop in the K–2 Classroom: Discovering Our VOICES*. Norwood, MA: Christopher-Gordon.

Character Cards

© 2003 by D. Rickards and S. Hawes from *Exploring Writing Workshop in the K–2 Classroom: Discovering Our VOICES.* Norwood, MA: Christopher-Gordon.

dad or mom	**giant**	**teacher**
witch or wizard	**police officer**	**alien**
doctor	**fire fighter**	**monster**

astronaut

cowboy

farmer

grandma or grandpa

queen or king

clown

mermaid

boy or girl

pirate

© 2003 by D. Rickards and S. Hawes from *Exploring Writing Workshop in the K–2 Classroom: Discovering Our VOICES.* Norwood, MA: Christopher-Gordon.

Object Cards

© 2003 by D. Rickards and S. Hawes from *Exploring Writing Workshop in the K–2 Classroom: Discovering Our VOICES.* Norwood, MA: Christopher-Gordon.

book	**tree**	**pencil**
paper	**pumpkin**	**school bus**
toothbrush	**fire**	**apple**

Spinners

Strong Verbs Spinner

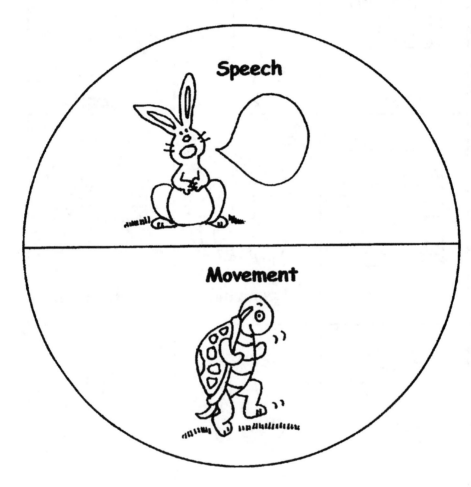

© 2003 by D. Rickards and S. Hawes from *Exploring Writing Workshop in the K–2 Classroom: Discovering Our VOICES.* Norwood, MA: Christopher-Gordon.

© 2003 by D. Rickards and S. Hawes from *Exploring Writing Workshop in the K–2 Classroom: Discovering Our VOICES*. Norwood, MA: Christopher-Gordon.

Leads Spinner

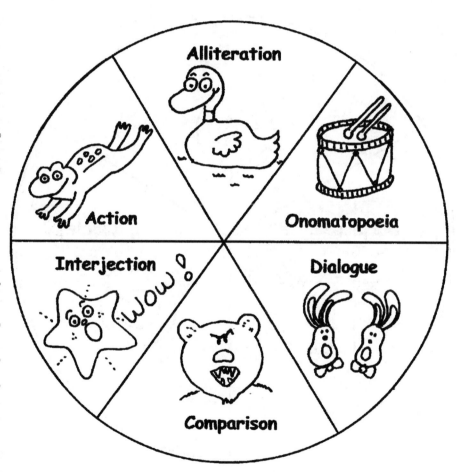

Endings Spinner

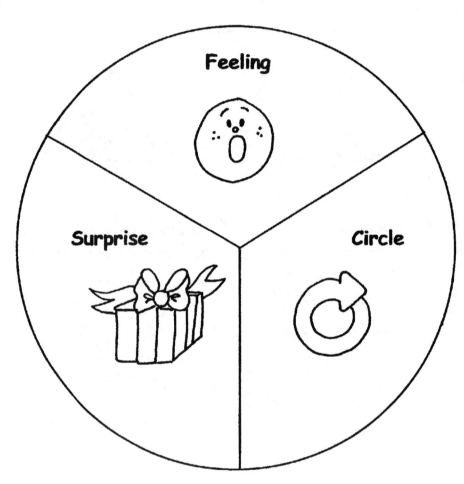

© 2003 by D. Rickards and S. Hawes from *Exploring Writing Workshop in the K–2 Classroom: Discovering Our VOICES.* Norwood, MA: Christopher-Gordon.

© 2003 by D. Rickards and S. Hawes from *Exploring Writing Workshop in the K–2 Classroom: Discovering Our VOICES.* Norwood, MA: Christopher-Gordon.

Alliteration Spinner

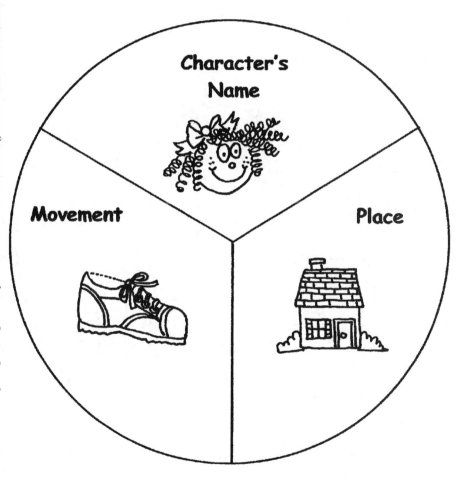

Comparison Spinner

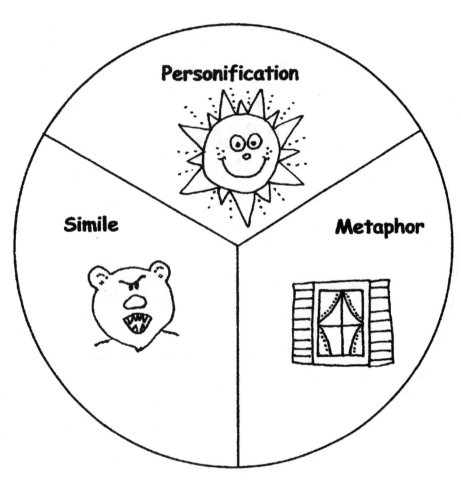

© 2003 by D. Rickards and S. Hawes from *Exploring Writing Workshop in the K–2 Classroom: Discovering Our VOICES*. Norwood, MA: Christopher-Gordon.

© 2003 by D. Rickards and S. Hawes from *Exploring Writing Workshop in the K–2 Classroom: Discovering Our VOICES*. Norwood, MA: Christopher-Gordon.

Emotions Spinner

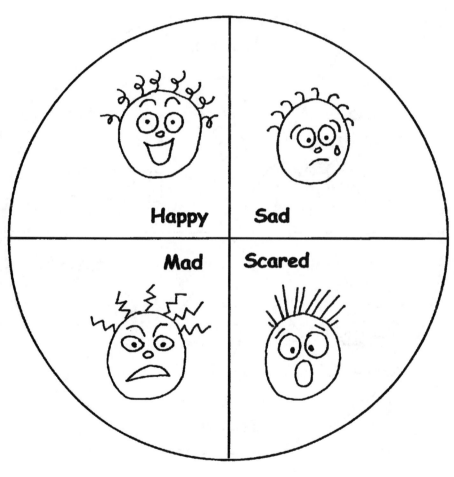

Descriptive Words Spinner

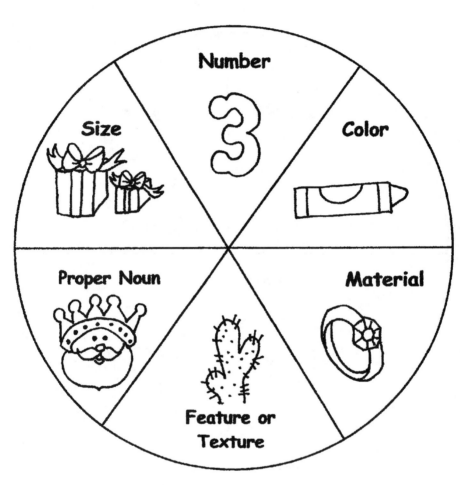

© 2003 by D. Rickards and S. Hawes from *Exploring Writing Workshop in the K–2 Classroom: Discovering Our VOICES.* Norwood, MA: Christopher-Gordon.

References

Cowley, J. (1980). *Mrs. Wishy Washy.* San Diego: The Wright Group.

Freeman, M. (1998). *Teaching the youngest writers: A practical guide.* Gainesville, FL: Maupin House.

Heller, R. (1998). *Fantastic! wow! and unreal!: A book about interjections and conjunctions.* New York: Puffin Books.

McKissack, P. (1986). *Flossie and the fox.* New York: Dial Books for Young Readers.

Numeroff, L. (1985). *If you give a mouse a cookie.* New York: Scholastic.

Pattou, E. (2001). *Mrs. Spitzer's garden.* San Diego: Harcourt.

Pilkey, D. (1996). *The paperboy.* New York: Orchard Paperbacks.

Polacco, P. (1998). *Thank you, Mr. Falker.* New York: Philomel Books.

Prelutsky, J. (1983). *The Random House book of poetry for children: A treasury of 572 poems for today's child.* New York: Random House.

Rickards, D., & Hawes, S. (2003). *Primarily writing: A practical guide for teachers of young children.* Norwood, MA: Christopher-Gordon.

Ringgold, F. (1991). *Tar beach.* New York: Crown.

Silverstein, S. (1974). *Where the sidewalk ends.* New York: Harper & Row.

Tannebaum, J. (2000). *Teeth, wiggly as earthquakes.* York, ME: Stenhouse.

Viorst, J. (1972). *Alexander and the terrible, horrible, no good, very bad day.* New York: Anthemeum.

Wood, A. (1982). *Quick as a cricket.* Swindon, Great Britain: Child's Play International.

Index

The Authors

Debbie Rickards is the literacy support specialist at Boone Elementary in the Alief Independent School District, Houston, Texas. She has taught in the elementary grades for over 25 years and also teaches graduate level literacy classes for the University of St. Thomas in Houston. She is author, with Earl Cheek, Jr., of *Designing Rubrics for K–6 Classroom Assessment* and the co-author of *Primarily Writing: A Practical Guide for Teachers of Young Children,* both from Christopher-Gordon Publishers. She received her Ph.D. from Louisiana State University in 1997.

Shirl Hawes is a Reading Recovery™ and first-grade teacher at Drabek Elementary in the Fort Bend Independent School District, Houston, Texas. She has taught primary grades for over 20 years in school districts across Texas. She is the co-author, with Laurie MacGillivray, of "'I Don't Know What I'm Doing—They All Start with *B*': First Graders Negotiate Peer Reading Interactions" published in *The Reading Teacher* in November 1994. With Debbie Rickards, Shirl co-authored *Primarily Writing: A Practical Guide for Teachers of Young Children* (Christopher-Gordon, 2003). She is a 2001 recipient of the Fulbright Memorial Fund Teacher Scholarship for study in Japan.